Advance Praise

R. Raj Rao has written on India's gay life for thirty years with wit, insight and incisiveness. He always factors in class and caste. Here is the quintessential Raj Rao in a book which is the climax of his work as India's first and only gay theorist worth reading.

—**Hoshang Merchant,**
Poet and Former Professor,
University of Hyderabad

Prof. Rao's book brings together the major concerns of Queer Theory with the often conflicted and conflictual sexual politics of his own native India, and in doing so he effortlessly starts up a lively and politically astute conversation between Western queer theory and literary practice and those practicing and critiquing the sexual mores and sexuality-debates in India. In equal measures knowledgeable and passionate about both ends of the conversation, this is an important and valuable contribution to our understanding of the politics of sex in a transcultural frame of reference where different voices, including the author's own, continually question and inflect each other. It is also a courageous book that does not shy away from contested territory and will challenge our ideas of what it might mean to be 'queer' in India or elsewhere.

—**Ingrid Hotz-Davies,**
Professor, Universität Tübingen

CRIMINAL LOVE?

CRIMINAL LOVE?

QUEER THEORY, CULTURE, AND POLITICS IN INDIA

R. RAJ RAO

⑤SAGE

Los Angeles | London | New Delhi
Singapore | Washington DC | Melbourne

First published in 2017 by

 SAGE Publications India Pvt Ltd
B1/I-1 Mohan Cooperative Industrial Area
Mathura Road, New Delhi 110 044, India
www.sagepub.in

SAGE Publications Inc
2455 Teller Road
Thousand Oaks, California 91320, USA

SAGE Publications Ltd
1 Oliver's Yard, 55 City Road
London EC1Y 1SP, United Kingdom

SAGE Publications Asia-Pacific Pte Ltd
3 Church Street
#10-04 Samsung Hub
Singapore 049483

Published by Vivek Mehra for SAGE Publications India Pvt Ltd, typeset in 11/14 pt Cambria by, Fidus Design Pvt. Ltd, Chandigarh, and printed at Saurabh Printers Pvt Ltd, Greater Noida.

Library of Congress Cataloging-in-Publication Data

Name: Raj Rao, R. (Ramachandrapurapu), author.
Title: Criminal love?: queer theory, culture, and politics in India/R. Raj Rao.
Description: Thousand Oaks, California: SAGE, 2017. | Includes bibliographical references and index.
Identifiers: LCCN 2017020155 | ISBN 9789386446497 (pbk.: alk. paper) | ISBN 9789386446503 (epub 2.0) | ISBN 9789386446510 (ebook)
Subjects: LCSH: Gays—India. | Gay rights—India. | Queer theory—India.
Classification: LCC HQ76.3.I4 R35 2017 | DDC 306.76/60954—dc23
LC record available at https://lccn.loc.gov/2017020155

ISBN: 978-93-864-4649-7 (PB)

SAGE Team: Rajesh Dey, Guneet Kaur Gulati, Shaonli Deb and Ritu Chopra

For Dibyajyoti Sarma

Bulk Sales

SAGE India offers special discounts
for purchase of books in bulk.
We also make available special imprints
and excerpts from our books on demand.

For orders and enquiries, write to us at

Marketing Department
SAGE Publications India Pvt Ltd
B1/I-1, Mohan Cooperative Industrial Area
Mathura Road, Post Bag 7
New Delhi 110044, India

E-mail us at **marketing@sagepub.in**

Get to know more about SAGE

Be invited to SAGE events, get on our mailing list.
Write today to **marketing@sagepub.in**

This book is also available as an e-book.

Contents

Preface

This book comprises three fundamental aspects of queerness relevant to us in India today—theory, culture, and politics.

Queer theory still largely comes to us from the West. We have yet to develop an indigenous queer theory of our own in India. Accordingly, some of the work of the most significant queer theorists of the 20th and 21st centuries, such as Michel Foucault, Eve Sedgwick, Jonathan Dollimore, Terry Goldie, Lisa Duggan, Judith Butler, Adrienne Rich, and Gayle Rubin, have been discussed in the book and applied to India. The Indian contribution to queer theory mainly consists of interpretations of Western queer theory by scholars like Brinda Bose, Pramod Nayyar, Ranjita Biswas, Akshay Khanna, Shohini Ghosh, Nivedita Menon, Niladri Chatterjee, and so on. This book follows in that tradition.

Queer culture in India has mainly been analyzed in the book through literature and film. The literature here includes references to my own work as a practicing writer, as well as to that of other contemporary writers. Chapter 8, the chapter on queer historiography, shows how gay and lesbian writing in India has been inadequately documented by literary historians, amounting thereby to a sort of censorship of the writers. It has been left to gay anthologists such as Hoshang Merchant, Ashwini Sukthankar, and Minal Hajratwala to correct the imbalance. Films, especially mainstream Bollywood films, also become a part of the discussion on Indian queer

culture. At the same time, there is an emerging gay and lesbian cinema in India that seeks to foreground the discrimination that queer people face. Of course, these films rarely have
successful commercial runs. They are usually confined to film
festivals.

This is a work of criticism, but it is the criticism of a practicing writer rather than that of a hard-boiled academic. Thus,
the views expressed are subjective, with all the drawbacks of
such an approach. The book by no means holds out an exhaus-
tive brief for Indian queer culture.

Queer politics in India has mainly revolved around Section
377 of the Indian Penal Code that criminalizes homosexuality.
Chapter IX, the longest chapter in the book, attempts a detailed
survey of this archaic law, introduced by the British in 1861.
The law involves all the three branches of the government—the
judiciary, the legislature, and the executive. It assumes special
significance in the light of the Supreme Court recriminalizing
homosexuality in India in December 2013, after overruling
a 2009 Delhi High Court judgment that read down the law.
It also assumes significance after the BJP, a right-wing Hindu
nationalist political party, came to power in May 2014. The book
highlights the irony in the stance of the courts and the government, which take the law to be a reflection of Indian culture
and values, stupidly overlooking the fact that it was actually
brought into force by the Victorians.

Another aspect of queer politics in India is the identity politics
that categories like gay, lesbian, MSM (men who have sex with
men, who may not identify as gay, and who often perform
heteronormative hierarchies in their sexual relations with
other men), transgender, and queer imply. These categories
have been discussed in the book. Alternative sexuality isn't a
monolith. Each identity category represents an ideology and
a way of life that differentiates it to some extent from other
categories. It is important for the reader to know this.

The focus of the book is contemporary India. My concern is principally with the 20th and 21st centuries. The historians Ruth Vanita and Saleem Kidwai have done seminal work on ancient and medieval same-sex love in India. Their book also has a section on modern India. But the selections included in their book mostly belong to the realm of literature. My work, though restricted to the last two centuries, attempts to go beyond literature.

The term 'queer' has been used in both a general (and generic) sense, as well as a specific sense in the book. In a general and generic sense, 'queer' has become an umbrella term to include diverse same-sex categories such as gay, lesbian, bisexual, MSM, transgender, and intersex. However, in a specific sense, the term 'queer' is the very antithesis of the word 'gay', as well as of categories like lesbian, MSM, transgender, and intersex. This is because queerness is concerned with the destabilizing of normativity, embracing the perverse, whereas the other categories mentioned previously desire to move towards the normative. Why this is so has been explained in the book. But it is for this reason that Vanita and Kidwai reject the prescriptive term 'queer' and opt instead for the descriptive term 'same-sex love'. To them, the word 'queer' has connotations that are unacceptable to Indians. Some researchers in India, open to the idea of destabilizing normativity, are nevertheless dissatisfied with the term 'queer', which they feel is a Western import. They suggest the use of alternative expressions to denote queerness, as for example the swear word *gaandu*.

Although the book deconstructs queer theory, culture, and politics in the Indian context, it does not place these aspects into watertight boxes. Of the nine chapters in the book, it is not as if there are three chapters each on queer theory, queer culture, and queer politics. Instead, there is an overlap. This is necessitated by the fact that the issues that the book takes up for scrutiny are interwoven. A theoretical formulation may be a throwback to a novel or a film, even as it puts into perspective the ramifications of the law. In turn, films and literature may be governed by the diktats of the law.

Academia in India has been known to club sexuality issues with gender issues, with disproportionate emphasis on the latter, possibly because, as an identity marker, gender has greater 'respectability' than sexuality. This book, like a handful of others before it, is an attempt to delink alternative sexuality from gender and establish it as an autonomous category. In doing so, one risks getting into conflict with the law. However, both as a practicing writer and as a queer theorist, I have been consistently opposed to the idea of self-censorship, foolhardy as that may appear.

R. Raj Rao
Pune
June 2017

Acknowledgments

Parts of this book first appeared in *Humanities Circle, The Critical Endeavour, Pune Times Mirror,* and in the edited volumes *Popular Masculine Cultures in India, Gay Subcultures and Literatures, De-stereotyping Indian Body and Desire* and *India Diversity.* Acknowledgement is due to the editors.

Introduction

This is a book that needs no introduction, but in the spirit of its defiant author here is one regardless. Novelist, poet, playwright, teacher, cinephile, polemicist, and public intellectual R. Raj Rao, stationed at the University of Poona, likewise needs no introduction, at least to the "us in India today" to whom he addresses these nine rousing essays. But perhaps a few words from an Indophile outsider will help contextualize these stirring interventions in the South Asian and global bodies politic, and ease the reader into the pleasurable but challenging experience of reading this book.

It has been all the more pleasurable for me since I have had the honor of being Raj's friend for at least a quarter century. I was one of only three Euro-American interview subjects in Rao's collection *Whistling in the Dark: Twenty-one Queer Interviews* (co-edited with another dear friend Dibyajyoti Sarma, 2009) as well as the addressee of the cryptically terse dedication of his potboiler novel *Hostel Room 131* (2010). In other words, the reader is warned that this introduction may feel like a combination of two films by another outsider Indophile, French director Louis Malle's *Phantom India* and *My Dinner with Andre*, a combination of voyeur ethnography and dinner table gossip. It will also feel layered over by echoes of the homosocial love duet from the 1970s megahit *Sholay*, "Yeh dosti" (this friendship), discussed at length by Rao in his illuminating essay on Indian same-sex friendship in the pages ahead.

Rao is, in my judgment, the most important contemporary queer Indian writer in English. One of the few Indian intelligentsia I know whose mother tongue is actually English, his mark on prose in that language is instantly recognizable, the poet erupting without warning whenever least expected. Rao denies he is "a hard-boiled academic," neither is he soft-boiled or scrambled, perhaps a masala omelette. He's certainly a skilled, erudite, and effective university teacher, for I've seen him in action many times with his engaged, intelligent, and adoring postgraduate students. His pedagogical voice is front and center throughout these essays, many of them caught up in the task of interpreting and popularizing classic Euro-American queer theory for the Indian reader. Much of that work—from Frenchmen Michel Foucault and Roland Barthes to American Judith Butler—is notoriously difficult, unfriendly, and often culturally and historically specific. But Rao rises to the challenge, cherry-picking those elements that are useful in the Indian context, negotiating those that need syncretizing with the South Asian heritage of sexual culture and theory—and, of course, rejecting those that are irrelevant to the postcolonial non-Judeo-Christian context.

Along the way, Rao sets up a fascinating and productive conversation between the queer theorists' 19th and 20th century European forebears, such as Oscar Wilde, André Gide, and Jean Genet, and their Indian political, cultural, and literary cousins, from the poet Hoshang Merchant to the brilliant historiographical duo, Ruth Vanita and Saleem Kidwai (who in 2000 provided Indian same-sex activists with a crucial tool in their pioneering paradigm-shifting anthology, *Same-Sex Love in India: Readings from Literature and History*). Incidentally, Rao's devoted attention to these peers and to dozens of other Indian artists in these pages declares that however unique and individualist his own voice may be, his essays embody a collective cohort and sensibility. Within this book, there are occasional overlaps and repetitions, a reminder both that the nine essays should not be read from start to finish in one sitting and that a good teacher always repeats the points to be learned for the exam. (You will not be given an exam once you have finished these essays, but the book will test you and make you take a stand.) As with any effective teacher also, Rao's tone fluctuates wildly, ranging from political outrage to prurient observation and confessional storytelling. The British critic, Oliver Ross, one of many who have given serious attention to Rao's novel *The Boyfriend*, has recently called his fiction "critique" and also uses the word "sardonic." These two descriptors are probably the most useful in describing *Criminal Love* as well. I wish I'd had Rao as a teacher myself.

In many ways, one of the most interesting and instructive chapters for a non-Indian is the one on homosociality. This category of male–male bonding, Eve Sedgwick, another English teacher, described in 1985 as both on a continuum with and in opposition to homosexual desire. She should have travelled to India rather than through 18th and 19th century English literature for her evidence. Suggesting that the culturally specific categories of "yaari" (friends) and "yaarana" (friendship) are a hallmark of Indian culture "that defines our bonding patterns globally," Rao's insider account identifies the ways male same-sex friendship within South Asian culture complicates the muddy landscape of sexuality and heterosexual marriage, in general, and the specifics of HIV transmission and gay relationships, in particular. (I first heard the word "yaar," when the *patka*-crowned members of the boys' football and hockey practice groups I was coaching at the Punjab Public School in the early 1970s would address each other in the heat of the battle as "yaar," but I didn't figure it out until I met Raj decades later and had poignant flashbacks of those fields of play and gender socialization.) While at first I was taken aback by the severity of Raj's moral judgments towards MSM and gay men who succumb to pressure and marry, several tragic stories he tells of the consequences for real people in the real world are chilling symptoms of the cultural impasse he is diagnosing. One is the famous 2010 incident where a gay professor at Aligarh Muslim University in Uttar Pradesh (UP), Dr Shreenivas Siras, was video-trapped in his own home by university authorities and recorded in an interclass same-sex dalliance. Siras was fired and he contested the outcome in court and won, but then committed suicide. The case resounded so strongly across the country that a fine Bombay feature film on the incident and its tragic outcome was made to positive notices in 2015. Rao recommended it to me and I was moved to tears (although I also wondered whether the Muslim rickshaw wallah "bait" should have not been given equal time). This eruption of hatred, violence, and shame within the academic universe that I love impacts me all the harder since I know that Western universities are not immune to such acts against nature as institutional lynchings. A case study elsewhere on the homosocial spectrum is a photograph I took of Raj and his then consort in 1999, seated discreetly a meter apart on a low wall, both in macho sunglasses, in front of a cinema in Panjim, Goa, as we waited to get in for the movie. Or rather they are the *ostensible* subject, for on the right of the two publicly anonymous, masculine-posing homosexuals, half a meter away, is another younger male couple, ostensibly heterosexual and homosocial, their limbs enlaced in each other's, and caught in a tender confidence and intimate conversation. I didn't realize my photograph caught unawares in one frame all of the contradictions and intensity of same-sex friendship that Rao unravels more than a decade later in *Criminal Love*.

Another illuminating yet chilling essay, the last and by far the longest in the book, "The Politics of Section 377, IPC," pertains to the recent political turbulence in India around the illegality of same-sex fucking. Rao's wonderful title for his collection surfaces out of this climactic chapter. The catchy phrase "Criminal Love" is also, according to Google, the title of songs by two unrelated pop singers, the Hawaiian J. Lauryn and the Swede Noonie Bao, an African-American serial novel by K. C. Mills, and a Russian-American short film, so the author is in good international company! In the queer context, the "criminal" has even more transcultural valence: soon after the High Court reversal, I went to Kashish, Bombay's queer film festival, and grabbed from the gift table an "I'm Cr[I'm]inal" T-shirt.

Its eventual Montreal recipient, a lucky AIDS activist, immediately put it on as an outcry against the proliferation of draconian legal sanctions around serostatus nondisclosure in the global North. This is not the first time that Indian queer discourses have been recycled in the West. In Rao's sense, "criminal" is no slogan nor a figure of speech but a historical fact, for his essay dissects the literal criminalization of same-sex intercourse by the infamous Section 377 of the Indian Penal Code over the last 150 years (except for a four-year interval, 2009–2013, thanks to the grace offered by the Delhi High Court, quickly overturned—also analyzed in depth by Rao). If you need the authoritative and definitive updating of this ongoing debacle and narrative, together with a fearlessly rigorous and

detailed analysis and cross-cultural, contextualized transhis-
torically—plus a provocative personal take—look no further.

One thrust of this fierce essay is that there's no going back.
The upheavals of the last decade, including the four years of
hope and the ongoing years of despair and frustration, have
changed the human landscape of queer India. This foreign
observer agrees, for I felt this everywhere in 2016 despite the
chill in the air drifting over allied struggles around minority
rights and civil liberties. Everywhere, from the bountiful
Bangalore Queer Film Festival, which involved everything
from frontal male nudity in performance art to onstage
bilingual banter (Tamil and Kannada) by hijra standup comic-
activists (and even films!), to Hyderabad Pride where I marched
surrounded by a strong contingent of beautifully adorned
hijras and one gay male friend's proud Goan mother, to
Chowpatty Beach where a large unauthorized demonstration
included jugglers, friendly tolerant cops, and a Hindi version
of "We Shall Overcome" that moved me to tears (again!), to
Juhu Beach where the Pride Tea Dance featured hundreds of
smart, young twenty-somethings so intent on their perfect
haircuts that they totally ignored this white-bearded Santa-
resembling *gora* with his sack of presents.... Of course, the
reader will respond: yes, middle-class Bangalore, Hyderabad,
and Bombay are one thing, but what about Saharanpur and
Hubli, and the villages beyond? In 1999, I reflected aloud
in a book chapter on Lawrence Cohen's concept of middle-
class metropolitan movements and identities. MMMIs are
still alive and well, of course, but the internet has blown
earlier configurations out of the water, including the binary
of metropoles and rural regions. Provincial conservatism and
traditional patterns are still deeply entrenched and enforced,
especially in places without internet access, and Rao provides
many perturbing anecdotal case studies to prove it. But there
can be no doubt that a paradigm shift is occurring, if unevenly
and haltingly, as any horny foreign net surfer who has met

ephemeral or steady virtual partners from Saharanpur and Hubli, live and canned, can attest.

Another thrust of Rao's discussion is less triumphalist and as sardonic and self-reflexive as we might expect. In this, he echoes the counter-homonormative critiques that have been festering in the West for a couple of decades now. These are getting louder and louder as the scary new age of Trump dawns. Rao is clearly on the same page as certain tendencies in the West. I am thinking, for example, of the US-Canadian collective "Against Equality," (http://www.againstequality.org/) whose slogan "Queer challenges to the politics of inclusion" and campaigns against energy-draining battles for same-sex marriage, military eligibility, and hate crimes legislation are in harmony with Rao's argumentation. He may well be right that legalistic solutions are ultimately less important than radical subversion from within. His pleasure in the Supreme Court's 2013 recriminalization of acts against nature, because he prefers the outlaw status thereby conferred on him, may seem like perverse rhetoric, but we all need a reminder of the arbitrariness and incompleteness of legal protection and of the urgency of deep cultural change.

Rao's stances may feel impulsive and rhetorical but are always calculated and very self-aware: Rao does not hesitate to acknowledge that his fight is "utopian." This is a word that needs reclaiming in both east and west, north and south. The late José Munoz anticipated Rao in this urgency:

> ...queer politics, in my understanding, needs a real dose of utopianism. Utopia lets us imagine a space outside of heteronormativity. It permits us to conceptualize new worlds and realities that are not irrevocably constrained by the HIV/AIDS pandemic and institutionalized state homophobia. More important utopia offers us a critique of the present, of what is, by casting a picture of what *can and perhaps will be*. (p. 35)

Along the way, Rao comes back again and again to the role of devil's advocate; for example, his argument elsewhere that Indian culture is less homophobic but simply corrupt and class-skewed is provocative but plausible. Do not come to these essays with certainties not open to questioning.

I was first introduced to Raj in 1992 by my British friend, the film scholar Richard Dyer, after he had finished a visiting fellowship at the University of Warwick. We soon arranged a meeting in India and struck a chord of mutual empathy and understanding. I had just read his story "Moonlight Tandoori," a tale of exile and lust set in a cheap takeout curry joint that probably captured more of his stay in England than any travel diary could have, and what is more, it turned me on. I knew that this was a voice and an imagination that I wanted to keep in close touch with, both professionally and personally. Thereafter my memories of our adventures together on two continents, both professional and personal, are ineradicable. How many of his boyfriends and partners have I got to know (among them the prototypes for Raj's fictional protagonists— Milind, Sandesh, and Ashutosh—not to mention nonfictional and pseudonymous Narendra and Dilip from *Whistling*), and how many he of mine? And how astutely?—Raj met and did not take long to stare into the soul of my hairy Brahmin scholar motorcyclist from Madhya Pradesh, who looks a little like a six-foot-three Akshay Kumar, and pronounce that he would be married within a year ... correctly. How many times have I visited his Department of English and presented to his students? One of the highlights of our professional relationship came exactly a decade ago when we organized together a three-day conference on the Poona campus called *Queer Literature and Cinema: The Canadian and Indian Experience*, and much real dialogue and exchange, understanding and misunderstanding ensued. Our personal relationship was no less often immortalized in photography. More than once he and I and Sandesh posed on a swanky restaurant terrace jutting out from one of Poona's hills, producing low-angle shots of us imitating DiCaprio and Winslet (and an even tackier Canadian diva than myself named Dion) against a railing that is uncannily prow-shaped. "My Heart Will Go On." Another time I introduced Raj to his first taste of snow in an April woodland in Quebec, and that moment offered less photographic glamour to posterity. Another winter we walked hurriedly late one night from one club to another in Montreal's bustling Gay Village: our destination was close by but not close enough to head off loud complaints that his ears were so literally freezing that they were about to snap off (but fortunately all other appendages were intact).

Needless to say, I am especially fond of *Criminal Love*'s confessional moments, for example, Raj's vivid accounts of his being smashed around in the Victoria Terminus toilets by blackmailing cops who he remembers as strangely complicit and non-homophobic once they got his money. This reminded me of the tour he gave me years earlier of Poona's cruisiest public loos back in the 1990s, filthy and foul-smelling spaces of freedom in comparison to the queer normativity that is going on in the 21st century, symbolized in his creepy anecdote about a casteist appeal for a Brahmin same-sex husband in the weekend matrimonial want ads. Raj has legendary scatological tendencies and familiar obsessions with public toilets and shit. Now that the orders that be in Delhi are calling for an end to public defecation, let's not be shy about this four-letter word immortalized by Raj in several of his poems, including his lyric guide to Bombay which the municipal tourist office should add to its visitors' literature:

Fumes shit pavbhaji
Skyscrapers local trains rats
Amitabh Bachchan.

In a recent as yet unpublished poem, he writes

But now the commuters
have been deprived of the joy of looking

by the state excelling in bans
which in the name of cleansing
has banned the squatters
from displaying themselves on the railroad tracks,
building washrooms for them in the dirty slums.
Now the killjoy state
has warned the men of dire consequences
if they crap in the open.

"Shivaling Swayamwar"

The blurb for the 2001 edition of his 1995 story collection tells it all, coy euphemisms notwithstanding, and anticipated how these filthy essays of 2017 would go against the grain of today's hygienically clean assimilationist platforms:

brash colloquialisms... the intertwining of the libidinal and political economies in supple, richly idiomatic prose.... suddenly you are jolted by an electric shock... a scorpion's sting... sulphurous... their fumes are the healthy scent of a corrupt and vital society, the disgust they evoke is a reaction to truth and must move any reader to thoughts of action.

But the confessional tone of those stories and these essays pushes things even further. Raj's nostalgic memories of cuddling and philandering among the stalls of pre-multiplex cinema halls in his youth are poignantly revelatory of the contradictions and pleasures of Indian orchestrations of masculine desire and sociality. As usual, confessionality creates both relationships and further confessions:

I too once upon a time got picked up in the front rows of a crowded Indian cinema. As I recall it was a sold-out afternoon show of the Kathakali biopic *Vanaprastham* in Calicut in 2000 and the gorgeous young film fan with whom I dallied for the next week at the Sea Queen Hotel was named Shaji if I'm not mistaken and he had a tongue as perky as a gecko's.

But I digress: such reminiscences are recounted only to corroborate my friend Raj's ethnographic research.

Much of the Waugh-Rao friendship has unfolded in the company of Rao the poet (unfortunately not represented in this volume of prose). I have to confess that I am not a regular poetry reader (though a few of my best friends are poets), but Raj's are the exception, terse and pithy personal pronouncements that provoke silence at his public readings and grab me deeply. The short film adapted from his "Bomgay" poems in 1996 by the late Riyad Wadia remains one of my favorite Indian films, and is undeniably a key, pioneering work in the contemporary Indian queer imaginary, despite it never having had an official release. If anyone doubts that Rahul Bose's pectorals are hot enough to fry eggs on, see this film. Many of Rao's poems will be associated forever with our confessional relationship. When my university brought Raj to Montreal in 2008 for a visiting scholar gig involving readings from his work, Raj produced a series of haikus. Most expressed the many normal cultural microshocks that every migrant faces but to which natives are often oblivious—from being called a "Paki" by some ne'er-do-well while smoking on a street bench (in a cosmopolitan city with more than 50,000 South Asian residents and almost 150 Indian restaurants?), to the experience of a female Québécois haircutter by a migrant whose experience of haircutting is indissociable from the homosocial erotics of Indian "saloons." The haiku concisely exploring this particular castrating shock is called "Barber Shop":

Haircut is a time
When I dream of dicks. Here I'm
Scissored by blonde chicks.

Rao's cutest Montreal haiku came out of the day I dragged him with a group of friends to our local gay nude beach at Oka. Of course, the South Asian culture that gave us the *Kama Sutra* is profoundly shaped by contradictory protocols that allow much class-determined public skin—in strictly controlled circumstances—but absolutely no public genital nudity, even in same-sex institutional showers. No surprise that South Asian travellers must often go through some serious acculturation before feeling comfortable in Euro-American nudist environments. Leave it to Rao to have sardonically overstated this challenge, dramatically overdraped with so much outerwear, hoods, towels, and scarves on that scorching summer day that from a distance he looked like a figure in a burka amid all those gleaming naked bodies on the beach. In the haiku "Nude Beach," rather than comparing the experience to being plunged among the naked sadhus at the Kumbh Mela, Rao got his revenge for my having tested him:

> *Water, sun and sand.*
> *Old men and their catamites.*
> *Size does not matter.*

I hope he is not referring to me in either line 2 or 3, but one never knows with poets.

I'm not sure about "catamite" but with regard to "chicks," few Western editors would allow this word, considered sexist, infantilizing, and pejorative according to feminist standards of course, except where used between scare quotes in an act of insider reclamation, as in B. Ruby Rich's wonderful volume of feminist film criticism *Chick Flicks.* Raj has no such privilege, and in fact his delight in using politically incorrect language throughout his poetry and in this book is legendary. Each one of Rao's sentences declares the destabilizing politics of language, and he is unapologetic. Witness the tongue-and-cheek disclaimer to the *One Day* collection: "The characters—and even narrators—in these stories are often politically incorrect. I apologise on their behalf." Even place-names are political (by this point the reader will have noticed that I am adopting Rao's stubborn practice of referring to Indian place names by their now superseded European-transliterated toponymy—from Poona to Bombay to Calicut to Panjim to

Bangalore. My refusal of Pune, Mumbai, Khozikode, Panaji and Bengaluru, etc., is not necessarily so much a parroting of Raj's thumbed nose at nationalist right-wingers who use symbolic semantic games to distract from their deeper agendas, but rather a homage to my friend's beau geste of the championing of lost causes, risk-taking and unsettling language.) Lesbians, in particular, will need to take several deep breaths in Rao's essay devoted to lesbian literature in India, but where else can we access such a knowledgeable, thorough, and thoughtful parsing of this corpus? And in any case, in the spirit of post-2013/14 turbulence, resistance, and coalitional volatility, most generalizations, including my preceding sentence, must be qualified if not confronted and reconstructed.

A final warning before you start your cruise as a reader through this book. Rao is a cinephile born and bred (having been brought up across the street from Bombay's Liberty Cinema), and the book is larded with cinephile references. Film fandom is another of our links, and Rao's inspired exegesis of scenes inspired the couple of essays I myself have published on Bollywood and Indian parallel cinema. If Amitabh is not a household word for you dear reader (which is of course impossible for any reader among "us in India today"), have a gander at *Sholay* before proceeding any further in this book. Rao is part of a generation of queer South Asian thinkers and writers, both *desi* and diasporic, from Shohini Ghosh to Gayatri Gopinath, for whom the cinematic imaginary is indissociable from the landscape of political and cultural struggle. That four of Rao's essays contain discussions of Deepa Mehta's 1996 Indo-Canadian feature film *Fire* is but a symptomatic reminder of the centrality of the cinema to the Indian body politic (in what other country do discussions of the latest cuts by the Central Board of Film Certification come up at every dinner table conversation and do cinemas get sacked by raging ideological mobs?), and of how this queer masterpiece marked the epoch that Rao is excoriating, teasing, and celebrating in these essays. Thus "cinematic" is just another word to add to the pile of epithets for this wonderful book by our perverse and prolific, prophetic and prurient Poona wallah politico-poet-pedagogue.

Thomas Waugh
Montreal
June 2017

Sex, Sexuality, Gender, and Culture

In Judith Butler's famous formulation, gender is performance. Butler calls gender a performative gesture (Butler, 1990: 25), and echoes Simone de Beauvoir who said that one was not born but became a woman (de Beauvoir, 1950: 122). The formulations of both de Beauvoir and Butler, of course, emphasize the social construction of gender. What these formulations seek to question, at one level, is the linguistic interchangeableness of the words—man/woman and male/female—in everyday speech. Eve Sedgwick seeks to avoid the confusion by introducing her concept of 'chromosomal sex' to distinguish biological sex from gender. Sedgwick says that the sentence "I can only love someone of my own sex" is wrong. It should actually be "I can only love someone of my own gender" (Sedgwick, 1990: 28). The meaning of the word 'sex' in such a sentence would refer to the prevalence of X and Y chromosomes in one's genetic makeup, and would possibly imply that one can only love a person who shares his or her exact chromosomal makeup.

If gender is a performative gesture, can the idea be extended to sexuality? Can we say that sexuality, and especially heterosexuality, is also a performative gesture based on performance? One obvious difference here would be that just as the performative aspect of gender applies more to women than to men ("I was not born a woman but became one"), the performative aspect of sexuality applies more to men than to women. This is because it is the man who is in possession of the penetrative organ, the penis, through the aid of which he enters (colonizes) the woman. This of course recalls the American feminist Andrea Dworkin (Dworkin, 1987) but what I am really concerned with is erection as a precondition to penetration. Now erection is an involuntary rather than a voluntary act. It may happen when a man least wants it to happen, and stubbornly refuse to happen when a man wants it to happen. The autonomous existence of the penis has frequently been referred to in literature. In Salman Rushdie's *Midnight's Children*, for example, the ayah says of the young Saleem Sinai, that his thing has a life of its own (Rushdie, 1982: 148). Erections not taking place when they ought to has a medical name for it. We call the syndrome 'erectile dysfunction', and the Bombay-based sexologist Dr Prakash Kothari has often revealed in newspaper and magazine interviews that over half of Indian men suffer from temporary or permanent erectile dysfunction. The male penis thus is not just a penetrative organ, but a performative organ as well. Performance, fundamentally, is a theatrical attribute, and it is interesting how the word 'climax' refers to both the high point of a five-act Shakespearean play and the high point, or orgasmic moment, of sexual intercourse. Thus, a biological male child must grow up to become a man, the word connoting not merely the heroic values of strength and courage, but also the ability to *get it up*. In the expression "So-and-so is not man enough," for example, a likely meaning of the sentence, depending of course on the context, is that he is impotent.

I call sexuality a social construct because it is society that expects a male (a state of being) to grow into a man (a state of becoming). Furthermore, such obligations are more incumbent upon the self-identified heterosexual man, rather than on the self-identified homosexual man, who, potentially at least, is freed of the obligation to perform by virtue of his non-normative sexual orientation.

However, the word homosexuality is not a monolith. We all know that there are plural same- sex identities that exist in the world today. Homosexuality existed long before the invention of the term 'homosexual' in the 19th century. Foucault thus relies on the word 'sodomite' to refer to the homosexuals of ancient Greece, but the word connotes at least as much as it denotes. What it connotes is the need of the homosexual subject to penetrate, regardless of the gender of the object. Penetration was equated with freedom (patriarchal male privilege) and with morality. In Foucault's words, "It was *immoral* for a *free* man to be *fucked*" (Lotringer, 1996: 364; emphasis mine). The sodomites of ancient Greece may have been homosexually inclined, but they sought sexual gratification in stereotypical rather than creative ways. They used their bodies as they thought they were designed to be used. On the other hand, their object choice, whom they penetrated or fucked, was, naturally, neither *moral* nor *free*. He was a slave. He was also a boy (as opposed to a man) which implies he was underage. In a supreme twist of irony, then, the onus of de-stereotyping the body, which Foucault equates with creativity, rested on the slave and the boy. The slave and the boy, unlike the sodomite, deconstructed the idea of sexuality as performance, because he was never the penetrator.

The sodomite of ancient Greece may be said to have his counterpart in modern-day India in the MSM community. MSM stands for men-who-have-sex-with-men (see Chapter II). MSMs do not want to be referred to as 'homosexual' or 'gay' even though they are attracted to people of their own sex (gender). MSMs wish to be a part of the mainstream, as a result of which they get married and produce children. They keep their MSM identities hidden from their wives and children throughout their lives, and thus end up leading 'double' lives. This is because marriage and the creation of a family do not automatically put a stop to their same-sex sexual activity. Post 1990, the MSM community in India has been thought to be the number one cause of the spread of acquired immune deficiency syndrome (AIDS), which they acquire from multiple male partners, and pass on to their wives. In a way, it is they who are responsible for the softening of the stand toward homosexuality on the part of the Government of India, which led to the reading down of Section 377 of the Indian Penal Code (IPC) in the Delhi High Court in July 2009. The government softened its stand, not because it is progressive, but because it wanted to contain the spread of AIDS by legalizing homosexuality (see Chapter IX).

But AIDS certainly is not the point of discussion here. We argue here that the MSM community in India, like the sodomites of ancient Greece, exercise their patriarchal privilege as *free* and *moral* citizens by not allowing their masculinity to be challenged in spite of their sexual attraction for their own gender. Notwithstanding their fantasies, they achieve this, among other things, by not allowing their bodies to be feminized during sex with other men (males) through a touch of their 'female' parts such as the nipples and the anus, which, for men, is the equivalent of the vagina. In other words, they always insist on the 'active' sexual role in bed, and a violation of this code on the part of their partners can even lead to homophobic violence (see Chapter II). Their 'passive' same-sex partners would be the equivalent of Foucault's slaves, who are *not* moral (in terms of social and ethical behavior) and *not* free (in today's terms, largely in the economic sense). They are often from the lowest rungs of the social order, excluded young males that society would identify as male prostitutes, or hijras. They are marginalized people for whom perverse sexual activity is frequently their only means of livelihood. But once again, ironically enough, it is these excluded men, rather than MSMs from the conservative middle class, who anti-essentialize the body.

Diana Fuss is of the view that homosexuality has its roots in patriarchy (Fuss, 1989). This, in a way, is proved by the sodomites of ancient Greece as well as by the MSM community of India, whose patriarchal homosocial bonding, and domination and oppression of women finds its objective correlative in latent homosexuality. What fosters the link, though, between patriarchy and latent homosexuality is homosociality, and this is equally true of ancient Greek society and modern Indian society. Homosociality implies a bonding that is nonsexual and is gender-specific rather than gender-neutral (see Chapter IV). It serves the interests of homosexuality by becoming its alibi. Thus in modern India, as in ancient Greece, men can establish non-genital physical contact with each other in public spaces, without arousing suspicion. Such nebulousness, incidentally, has all but disappeared from contemporary Western society, where the disappearance of homosociality has probably weakened the link between homosexuality and patriarchy. The sight of men holding hands, or walking with arms around each other's shoulders on Indian streets is too commonplace to be commented upon. But it sometimes leads to 'misunderstandings' among first-time Westerners in India, who wonder if all of India is like Castro Street in San Francisco, or Greenwich Village in New York City! Literature and cinema help us understand the concept of homosociality better. The post-Amitabh Bollywood film is full of instances of patriarchal homosocial bonding among men, as in the film *Satya*; this is also true of some regional cinema, such as Malayalam cinema. The first anthology of gay writing from India, edited by Hoshang Merchant, was appropriately called *Yaraana* (Merchant, 1999), but much before Merchant cashed in on the word *yaar,* Raj Ayyar, a contributor to the volume *A Lotus of Another Color: An Unfolding of the South Asian Lesbian and Gay Experience*, dwelt on the word *yaar* at length, and concluded that there is no word in the English language that can approximate it in breadth and meaning; not even the words 'friend' and 'buddy' which he calls "superficial" (Ratti, 1993: 169). *Yaar* then emerges as a culture-specific term that best describes the homosociality to be found in South Asia. That homosociality has also been written about by Pakistani-born British writer Hanif Kureishi in his essay "The Rainbow Sign," where Kureishi expresses his culture shock during his first ever visit to Pakistan, at the sight of Muslim men in tight embrace on the streets of Karachi and Lahore (Kureishi, 1986: 7–38). In my Introduction to my own book, *Whistling in the Dark: Twenty-one Queer Interviews*, I identify several male homosocial spaces in the public arena that give a fillip to patriarchy (Rao and Sarma, 2009: xx–xxi).

Because homosociality implies a nonsexual bonding, it enables closeted but practicing homosexual men, for whom sexuality is *not* an axis on which identity must be mapped, to establish an alibi of *yaari* that successfully serves to hoodwink family, friends, employers, neighbors, and society in general. It becomes a survival tactic that at once ensures that the homosexual subject is not repressed, and not persecuted by homophobic witch-hunters. In a sense, the homosexual subject here successfully manages to invert the hetero/homo binary, a point that I shall return to later, which is a necessary step in the deconstruction of the binary, as both Barthes and Derrida have argued (Sedgwick, 1990: 10). While he inverts the binary as a homosexual, however, he keeps it in place as a patriarch, more so if he is married. Surveys have indicated that the majority of homosexual men in India (including MSMs, as pointed out earlier) are married. The homosexual man's 'double' life, then, may be said to oppress his wife, more so as it is carried out in secret, without, as it were, keeping her in the loop. This is exactly what happens in Amol Palekar's Marathi film *Thaang* (its English version is called *Quest*). The writer of the film, Sandhya Gokhale (Gokhale, 2006), is a mainstream feminist who sees the narrative from the wife's point of view and castigates the husband; whereas I, as a queer theorist, see it from the husband's point of view and call him a victim.

The interface between patriarchy and homosexuality is thus complicated.

Homosociality cannot effectively function as an alibi for homosexual men without abetment by its comrade-in-arms, heterosexism. The concept of (hetero)sexism originally derives from feminist theory. Heterosexism may be said to be the hegemonic construction of heterosexuality through performativity. Sex, a biological construct, expresses itself through gender, a social/cultural construct (masculine/ feminine), and then through heterosexual desire which is projected as essential, natural, and universal. This compulsory heterosexualization of desire, a phrase made famous by Adrienne Rich (Sedgwick, 1990: 36) is responsible for the treatment of homosexual love as deviant and pathological. Heterosexism is widely prevalent in India on account of the obscuring of historicity, and scholars such as Ruth Vanita, Saleem Kidwai, Devdutt Patnaik, and Giti Thadani have done seminal work in an attempt to de-obscure history (see works cited). Simply said, heterosexism is the belief that sexual attraction is always gender specific, never gender neutral. That is to say, a biologically born male can only be sexually attracted to a biologically born female and vice versa. A biologically born male cannot be sexually attracted to another biologically born male; likewise, a biologically born female cannot be sexually attracted to another biologically born female. However, if homosociality provides the linkage between homosexuality and patriarchy, then heterosexism must be culpable too. In real terms, this was best proved in India in the year 1998, when the Hindu Right sought a ban on Deepa Mehta's lesbian film *Fire*. Ironically, the fieriest protests came from women rather than men. The men *did* make half-hearted noises, but eventually withdrew them in the knowledge that lesbian sexuality, when portrayed on screen, titillated them in a way that perhaps even heterosexual pornography did not. But the women went on record to vituperatively ask that "If women turn to each other to satisfy their [sexual] needs, what happens to the institution of the family?" Doubtless, this was a rhetorical question that implied two things. First, notwithstanding heterosexism, the protestors were aware of the fact that a biologically born female could, technically and potentially, be attracted to another biologically born female. Second, what scandalized them was if women gave expression to such 'deviant' desire, the institution of the family, one of the most solid manifestations of the patriarchy, would be under threat. The women who asked this question represented womankind at the opposite end of the feminist spectrum. They were co-opted by the patriarchy in so foolproof a manner as to be completely blind to the film's liberating possibilities; in spite of the fact that in all probability, the majority of them had husbands who had outside love interests, who regularly came home late, who drank regularly, and who regularly indulged in wife-beating. And that in Marathi, 'she' is the word for excrement.

The protests against the protestors were equally revealing. The lesbians who joined the marches against the banning of *Fire* were inverting the binary. However, the mainstream feminists who accused the lesbians of "hijacking" the protests (Sukthankar, 1999: Editor's Note) were, in a sense, keeping the hetero/homo binary in place. As such, the latter refused to call the film a lesbian film, and explained that the lesbianism portrayed in the film was at best 'situational' lesbianism, because the women in question were both married (they were actually sisters-in-law, which to some may even introduce an incest angle) and turned to each other only because their husbands did not sleep with them!

To my mind, nothing can be more simplistic. In a homosocial and heterosexist culture where no sex education worth its name exists, situations often allow people to discover their true sexual natures (in the chromosomal sense) and true sexual identities (in the homopolitical sense). The notion of situational or circumstantial homosexuality must thus be dismissed as a myth, or at least taken with a pinch of salt.

The women's wing of the Shiv Sena that protested against the screening of *Fire* was co-opted by patriarchy in real life, and this is exactly what happens in a 1970s Marathi film, *Umbartha*, directed by Jabbar Patel, in reel life. The film is set in a home for destitute women in rural Maharashtra. When two of them, one butch, the other femme, are caught making out on the roof one night, the other women, ironically, turn against them. Ironically because, as destitutes, one expects them to bond with anyone who is marginalized. As dinner is served in the community kitchen the next day, one of them suddenly flings a bowl of boiling hot dal on the butch lesbian and scalds her. A better instance of homophobia probably does not exist in Indian cinema.

Two 19th century writers, Andre Gide and Oscar Wilde, become focal points in any discussion on de-stereotyping the body and desire. Both were homosexual, but their approach toward their homosexuality was poles apart. Gide was steeped in his religion, Christianity, which he must have found difficult to reconcile with his homosexuality. He accepted his homosexuality as natural to him, and as his essential identity, but in the conservative heteronormative environment in which he lived in 19th century Europe, his method was to downplay it, to not be loud about it, and perhaps to even abstain from sexual activity altogether. This is what brought him into conflict with Oscar Wilde. When they once met by chance in a foreign country, Algiers, Wilde tempted Gide to transgress by introducing him to a very handsome Muslim sex worker, Mohammed. Gide spent the night with Mohammed in a state of absolute bliss, but the next morning he was overcome by guilt—he had sinned, and doubtless, the man responsible for it was Oscar Wilde. He wrote a letter to his mother, in which he described Oscar Wilde as "a most dangerous product of modern civilization" (Dollimore, 1991: 5). But this is exactly how Wilde liked to be described. Wilde anticipates Foucault through his anti-essentialist approach that made him equate his homosexuality with transgression. Sexual transgression was but a stage in Wilde's development of his transgressive aesthetic and political homosexuality. Wilde's trials that led eventually to his death are legion, but the trials were as much on account of his sexual transgression as his aesthetic and political transgression. Wilde substituted moral attributes, such as truth, sincerity, and maturity which society held in high esteem, with their opposite—lies, insincerity, and narcissism. In this, he was similar to another gay writer, Jean Genet. Homosexuality, to Wilde and Genet, outlawed by the church and the state, and pathologized by medicine, could never be a part of one's essential identity, as Andre Gide believed. The only viable option left to the homosexual, then, was to transgress. Transgression, here, amounted to sexual perversion as well as the belief in radical views expressed through literature that went against society's established norms. Both Wilde's *The Picture of Dorian Gray* and Genet's *A Thief's Journal* belong to this category of literature. As for sexuality, perversion has many forms; but for the homosexual, the one form of sexual activity that is ideologically ruled out is monogamous vaginal sex with the woman one is married to, that is practiced not for pleasure but procreation. All other forms of sexual activity, arguably, have pleasure as their main aim. Thus, it is through perversion (see Chapter VII) that a successful de-stereotyping of the body is achieved.

At this point, I must return to Foucault. In his interview referred to earlier, Foucault says, "Not to be gay is to limit the effects of my choice in such a way, that my life does not change in any significant manner." Earlier in the sentence, Foucault also says that, "It is not necessary to be homosexual, but it is necessary to be set on being gay." To Foucault, being gay is tantamount to "being creative of ways of life" (Lotringer, 1996: 369–70).

What does Foucault's distinction here between 'gay' and 'homosexual' mean? Foucault uses the term homosexual in an essentialist sense to indicate a sexual preference and a sexual identity, such as that possessed by Andre Gide. On the other hand, he uses the word 'gay' in an anti-essentialist sense, the sense in which Oscar Wilde was gay. The homosexual man or woman who is convinced that homosexuality for him/her is an axis on which identity can be mapped and/or is a natural sexual preference, effects a simple inversion of the hetero/homo binary. Such a person may be said to substitute heteronorma-tivity with homonormativity. In doing so, the homosexual sub-ject resorts to appropriation, no doubt, but it is an appropriation combined with transformation. Within the homosexual sub-culture, the homosexual subject has transformed 'homo' from a position of victimhood to a position of empowerment. This, however, leads to stasis; it does not amount to a successful dis-mantling of the status quo. If homophobia is the concomitant of heteronormativity, then the concomitant of homonorma-tivity may be said to be heterophobia. The binary, rather than being displaced, continues to exist, albeit in inverted form. Literary theorists differ on the importance of inverting the binary as a necessary stage in its displacement. While Barthes prefers to skip the stage, and head straight for utopia, Derrida sees inverting the binary as a crucial way station in its decon-struction. In Foucault's view, a gay man is a homosexual who uses his homosexuality to perceive the world differently. The different perception, then, amounts to exercising free choice in a way that is not conducive to maintaining the status quo. This includes a change in lifestyle, especially in the sexual sense, that gives the gay man a veritable carte blanche to live as debauched a life as he pleases (as perhaps Foucault himself did). I say 'gay man', because the lesbians were not so sure. Their sympathies were still with the feminists, though in the post-AIDS world, they were written off by the feminists who regarded them as no different from gay men, whose promiscu-ity had given the world AIDS. However, residues of their love affair before AIDS still lingered. At that time, in Sedgwick's picturesque phrase, "Feminism is the theory, lesbianism is the practice" (Sedgwick, 1990: 36). The lesbians were not as 'moral' as the feminists, but they still preferred the stability of relationships to the destabilizing reverberation of normativity, as advocated by queer theory. The result was that the lesbian project all over the world branched off in a somewhat different direction from that taken by gay men. For lesbians today, the interface of gender and sexuality remains a much more pertinent issue than it does for male queer theorists. This is manifested, for example, in diametrically opposed attitudes that the former and the latter may have toward issues such as pornography and pedophilia. In my own experience, lesbians are unwilling to make any compromises, especially with regard to pedophilia. Literature and cinema on the subject that could once be freely discussed, such as Thomas Mann's *Death in Venice* (1971, director Luchino Visconti) or the Canadian film *Montreal Main* (1974, director Frank Vitale) are today suspect. Organizations like NAMBLA (North American Man Boy Love Association) are thoroughly discredited by feminists and lesbians alike, and are today outlawed.

I would argue that the phrase "de-stereotyping body and desire" is a similar formulation to Wilde's anti-essentialism, as analyzed by Dollimore, to Derrida's idea of deconstructing the binary, and to Foucault's view that equates gayness to creative lifestyle change. One contemporary scholar who comes across to me as a disciple of Wilde and Foucault is the York University professor of English, Terry Goldie. Terry Goldie's book *Queersexlife* (2008) is an amalgam of scholarship and pornography. The author takes a close look at his own life, at his own sexual life to be precise, and deconstructs his own sexual behaviors and practices that range from cross-dressing to fathering children to being anally penetrated by men. In the end, it is impossible to pinpoint the real, or the essential, Terry Goldie. Just when we begin to think Terry Goldie is homosexual, he surprises us by revealing that he was "born to be a parent," (Goldie, 2008: 10) and what is more, has actually produced children. If we think of him as heterosexual, then, he says he is not that either, because he has the best orgasm when he is anally penetrated by another man. This may lead some of us to describe him as "passive." But Terry Goldie prefers to think of himself as "active" because, he says, he uses his penis in exactly the same way that other men do. That is to say, he has erections and ejaculates just like other men, but unlike them, does not ejaculate in a vagina, but masturbates and ejaculates *as* he is being penetrated by another man. Eve Sedgwick calls masturbation "autoerotic sex," (as opposed to sex with another person, which she calls "alloerotic sex"; Sedgwick, 1990: 25–26). Sedgwick suggests that autoerotic sex has so many practitioners all around the world, that she wonders why the sexuality binary is not made up of alloerotic/autoerotic, instead of hetero/homo. Terry is a man's name. Though Terry Goldie wears his hair long and usually dresses in men's clothing, that is, shirts and pants, which is to say that in terms of gender, he is socially and culturally constructed as a man, his book has photographs of him in an Indian sari, and in other female attire. The photographs look so real that it would be impossible for anyone who does not know Terry Goldie to say that they are of a man. Once again here, essence eludes the author.

The most anti-essentialist and creative part of Terry Goldie's book, however, is the chapter entitled "I Never Took it Up My Ass" (Goldie, 2008: 120–143). Here the author speaks of the time when he has sex with a woman but does not use his penis at all, which he uses when he has sex with men. Instead, both he and his female partner gratify themselves by using what Terry Goldie calls a "double-ended dildo." As the author describes his sexual practice, which is undoubtedly *creative* of ways of life, he becomes graphic, even pornographic, in his attention to detail. He says, one end of the double-ended dildo is inserted in his partner's vagina, and the other in his own anus. In doing so, the author successfully manages to feminize his body during sex with another woman, not another man. Heteronormativity, patriarchy, and masculinity are, thus, all destabilized at one go. Heterosexuality ceases to be a performativity gesture. The body becomes a site which, through its de-stereotyping, heralds change. But the change is no ordinary change. On the contrary, it is utopian. Foucault says, one cannot stabilize oneself in a position, including that of homosexuality. To Foucault and his followers, the key lies in destabilizing normativity, in toppling its stable foundations, and reducing it to rubble. Debris. That is why, according to one view, the sexuality revolution generates more power, more energy, than even the Great Wars.

Homosexuality has always been looked upon with disfavor by three agencies universal to mankind. The first of these is religion. Although attitudes to deviant desire vary from religion to religion, with some religions like Hinduism being less judgmental about it than others like Islam and Christianity. Religion, on the whole, believes that the purpose of human sexuality is procreation, which keeps the life cycle going. To religion, sexual activity is a means to an end, not an end in itself. To foreground the recreational aspect of sex, which in a sense is what homosexuality does, is to treat sex as an end in itself, as perhaps the animals do. But man, who has been gifted with reason, cannot afford to be like the animals. He must manage his sexual life responsibly, and he can only be said to do so when he practices procreative sex. Now, heterosexual sex alone is procreative, and even though heterosexuals do not always have sex to reproduce, heterosexuality must be given the benefit of doubt. Homosexual sex can never be procreative, unless science intervenes and makes this possible. But scientific inventions have rarely curried favor with religion that is orthodox by nature. If science makes it possible for a man to get pregnant, we can be sure that religions across the spectrum, rather than laud the achievement, will see it as the handiwork of the devil.

Then there is the law. Except for Plato's ideal republic, where human beings are so wise that they do not need laws to govern them, laws exist everywhere in the world. And the law, somehow, has always seen homosexuals as outlaws (perhaps because we cannot become in-laws). That is to say, if homosexuals are attracted to their own sex, they will not get married, and if they do not marry, they will not have fathers-in-law and mothers-in-law, and in turn will not be sons-in-law and daughters-in-law. In the West, laws have had to be amended to accommodate homosexuals—it is not as if they did not exist in the first place. In the East, laws differ from country to country, with some Muslim countries still having laws in their law books that make it mandatory for homosexuals to be stoned to death. In India, Section 377 has given the police a carte blanche to harass homosexuals, and the harassment can vary from blackmail to extortion to gay bashing that can even lead to death (see Chapter IX). In the 20th century, such crimes have been reported from countries as diverse as Iran on the one hand, and United States on the other.

Finally, there is medicine. Medicine, with its overemphasis on biology, has always pathologized homosexuality, taking it to be a disorder. Like religion, medicine disapproves of homo-sexuality because it thinks it to be against nature's purpose, which is to ensure that the species reproduce. In America, it took a great deal of brainwashing by gay activists to get the American Psychiatric Association to knock off homosexuality from its list of mental disorders. But hardly did they succeed when AIDS made its appearance and got the medical frater-nity worked up once again. Doctors saw AIDS as a gay disease. Some of them even went on to suggest that AIDS, with its pain-ful symptoms, was the punishment meted out to homosexuals for perverse sexual behavior. In turn, many homosexual men became subscribers to a 'conspiracy theory' that AIDS was a cunning invention of doctors who wanted to foist expensive medicines manufactured by multinational drug cartels on unsuspecting homosexuals, some of them with seemingly huge disposable incomes. Yet, in those early days, AIDS medicines, when they arrived in the market, were so phenomenally expensive that they were out of reach of most homosexual men.

Homosexuality is not peculiar to mankind. It exists among other forms of life as well. National Geographic Channel once telecast a program that showed animals indulging in gay behavior. As far as human beings are concerned, homosexuality was practiced by the ancient Greeks and Romans. Although, as stated earlier, it was not called homosexuality then. It was called sodomy. Homosexuality was also known (and practiced) in ancient and precolonial India. The one text, of course, that proves this is the *Kamasutra*, which frequently refers to the 'third sex'. Then again, there is Khajuraho in Madhya Pradesh. Hinduism has many homosexual myths and legends involving our gods and goddesses. In colonial India, two poetic forms were supposed to have been distinctly gay. One was the ghazal, where men wrote love lyrics to men. The other was *rekhti* poetry, where men assumed the personae of women and wrote erotic verse to them (Vanita and Kidwai, 2000).

The terms 'homosexual' and 'heterosexual' first made their appearance in the 19th century. Ironically, the former term preceded the latter. This meant that heterosexuality was being understood in terms of homosexuality, and not the other way round. The Victorians foisted their quaint morality on us. Anything to do with sex scandalized the Victorians of the 19th century, and they bequeathed that mindset to us. In the 20th century, the majority of Indians were inheritors of that mindset. That we have a poor sense of history only contributed to our amnesia (or loss of memory) that made us forget the *Kamasutra* and Khajuraho. Today, Indians do not read the *Kamasutra*, and most of us do not even know where Khajuraho is.

Today, people across the spectrum in India, from politicians, corporates, and bureaucrats to the common man who travels in jam-packed trains and buses, think that homosexuality is against Indian culture. What we ought to realize, however, is that our myopic view of history makes the Victorians successful in their endeavor to erase our past. And this was not just about our sexual past. It was also about our linguistic past, as English replaced Sanskrit and the *bhashas*. Significantly, it was the same man, T. B. Macaulay, who was behind both these moves.

All over the world, gay men are believed to have high disposable incomes. The reasons for this are obvious. Gay men are single. They are not encumbered with wives and children who drain their resources, leaving nothing for them to spend on themselves. Gay men often squander away their money instead of stashing it away. They worry that if they do not spend their money in their lifetime, it might pass into unknown hands after their death. The global economy sees a lucrative business opportunity in tapping the resources of gay men. The liquidity possessed by gay men is sometimes referred to as 'pink money'. The color pink, associated in the normative world with femininity, has been appropriated by gay men to challenge the stereotype. However, its real origins lie in the pink triangle that was worn around the necks of gay men by the Nazis of Germany. Businessmen invent profitable business propositions to earn a share of this pink money. Many major cities in the West have gay neighborhoods and gay districts that have shops selling gay merchandize. The merchandize varies from things such as rainbow flags to hardcore porn. It includes gay literature, gay films, and fashion accessories such as rings and tattoos to adorn different parts of the anatomy. The shops bustle with activity round the year, but do brisk business on special days like Gay Pride Day. Clients can be themselves in the stores; they do not have to furtively look around to make sure that no one sees what they buy. However, merchandize is not the only route to the gay man's purse. There is gay tourism that offers such attractive packages to gay clients, that they willingly swipe their credit and debit cards to enjoy a weekend of sheer bliss with their lovers at, say, a seaside resort.

As far as India is concerned, though we have a sizable gay population, none of the things described earlier exist so far. There are rich gay men with hefty bank balances, but there are no special gay districts in our metropolitan cities. Thus, there is no special gay merchandize. Nor does gay tourism exist in India.

Since many gay men happen to be rich, they have been victims of blackmail and extortion all over the world (see Chapter V). The culprits are either hoodlums, or unsurprisingly, the police themselves. They are thugs who go scot free, because if theft is a crime, so is homosexuality, at least technically. So, it is one criminal against another. What is the modus operandi of the gay blackmailer? He leads his victims on, pretending to be gay himself, and then makes an about turn, declaring himself to be a cat among the pigeons. Thus cornered, gay men are willing to pay the culprits any amount to secure their release, for to their way of thinking, this is preferable to the shame of being outed.

II

Identities

In my Introduction to my book *Whistling in the Dark: Twenty One Queer Interviews*, co-edited with Dibyajyoti Sarma, I define MSMs (Men Who Have Sex With Men) as follows:

> MSMs are those for whom sexual activity with persons of their own gender neither constitutes an identity nor a preference. At best they see it as a tendency, something they have got addicted to like tobacco or alcohol, and find it difficult to relinquish. Obviously, there is an implicit sense of denial in their stance, in their perception of themselves, that needs to be dealt with through counseling....
>
> (Rao and Sarma, 2009: xx)

Earlier, I talk about how many Indian men prefer casual sex with other men, rather than visits to female sex workers, because the former is free of cost, and the chances of their contracting sexually transmitted diseases are, in their view, less. What is important, however, is that the proportion of such men in relation to the total population is so high, that Indian queer theory cannot afford to ignore them. Though MSMs reject the notion of identity based on sexual desire, they have, over time, themselves come to constitute an identity and have added to the plethora of queer sexual identities already available in this country, such as gay, lesbian, bisexual, transgender, *koti, panthi,* hijra, and so on. In this chapter, I attempt to examine the social contexts conducive to the emergence of MSM identities, and study the impact of MSM behavior on masculinity.

Indian social life may be said to be significantly characterized by the segregation of the sexes, fostered mainly by the system of 'arranged' marriages (as opposed to 'love' marriages), prevalent in the culture since ancient times. Barring certain tribal communities, arranged marriages are a universal practice throughout the Indian mainstream. Morality is not the defining principle behind arranged marriages; rather, an arranged marriage is a safety valve that guarantees against intermarriage, especially in respect of caste, class, and religion. To this day, a Hindu–Muslim marriage still has the potential to foment a riot, particularly in provincial and small-town India.

Matrimonial advertisements, even in leading English daily newspapers such as *The Times of India,* openly endorse the idea of marrying within one's caste, more so if one is upper caste. A Brahmin–Dalit wedding (such as that portrayed in Vijay Tendulkar's Marathi play *Kanyadaan*) can be inflammatory. Cross-class marriages are so scandalous that short of the cross-class couple eloping, they are an impossibility, fit to be dealt with only in Bollywood movies, such as *Jab Jab Phool Khile* in the 1960s and *Raja Hindustani* in the 1990s. Arranged marriages are a sort of guarantee against such 'deviant' alliances, because the parents of the marrying couple are in the loop to make sure that there are no social transgressions taking place: the marriages are, as is well known, frequently between families than between individuals. In the Indian social context, the term 'love marriage' still has largely negative connotations and is associated in the public imagination with the act of eloping or running away.

What this, of course, proves is the Indian preoccupation with purism as opposed to hybridity, worsened by the late capitalism of the 1990s. A marriage in India must never be with the 'other', which explains why our marriages are almost entirely devoid of romance.

In such a scenario, how does an Indian male gratify his sexual desire? Clandestine sex with a girlfriend or prostitute or relative is one way out, but perhaps less complicated than this for the conundrums it can lead to is sex with another man, which in the heterosexist culture of India can easily pass for *yaari*. Two men can make out in a house in which the extended family, including parents, grandparents, brothers, sisters, uncles, aunts, and cousins is present, and they would be suspected of nothing. The family would think of the men as *yaars* and of the relationship as nonsexual (if at all sex comes to their mind), because sex after all cannot happen between two people of the same gender. Thus, MSM sexual activity is far less complicated than heterosexual sex for the natural alibi it provides. Many MSMs today lament that Bollywood blockbusters, like Karan Johar's *Dostana*, destroy their alibi by alerting family members to the possibility of a homosexual relationship. In the past, an all-encompassing innocence, naiveté even, prevailed, which movies like *Dostana* have the potential to expose.

In the late 1940s and early 1950s, a report known as the Kinsey Study Report on Human Sexuality made its appearance in America. The study shocked the world. Till then the belief was that human beings were either heterosexual or homosexual—nothing less, nothing more. The Kinsey Study rejected this belief. It claimed that human sexuality existed on a six-point scale, with heterosexuality at one end of the scale and homosexuality at the other end. The in-between positions on the scale represented varying degrees of bisexuality. The study radicalized thinking on sexuality because it implied that exclusive heterosexuality, which was thought to be near-universal, was, in fact, as rare as exclusive homosexuality. The vast majority of human beings, by this formulation, were bisexual.

The Kinsey Study was genetics based. It arrived at its conclusions on the basis of the fact that the hormonal and chromosomal makeup of human beings differed from individual to individual. Thus, it was incorrect to presume that there were only two sexualities, heterosexuality and homosexuality. There was a third sexuality—bisexuality—that was not as rigid as heterosexuality and homosexuality. Instead, it covered a whole range of midpoints on the scale that suggested that there were multiple kinds of bisexuality itself. There were human beings who were mainly attracted to people of their own sex, and they were bisexual. And there were human beings who were mainly attracted to people of the opposite sex, and they too were bisexual. The two kinds of bisexuality were different in degree, though not in kind. The Kinsey Study Report brought out the hypocrisy of human society vis-à-vis homosexuality. If merely one-sixth of the population was homosexual, then merely one-sixth of the population was heterosexual too. It was thus unfair to discriminate against homosexuals and pass laws that were disadvantageous to them.

It is the prevalence of bisexuality that makes it possible for men to have sex with men when they are segregated from women. This happens, for example, when men are in prison, or when they are posted to 'non-family' stations in the army, navy or air force, or when boys study in boarding schools and live in dorms. It also happens in India where the system of 'arranged marriage' keeps men and women apart until their families find them spouses. The term 'queer' emerged as an umbrella term to include all forms of non-normative (and perhaps non-procreative) sex. Bisexuality is included in its ambit. Thus, bisexual people are also queer.

Same-sex sexual activity triggered by the segregation of the genders has often been described as 'situational' or 'circumstantial', and is not thought to be homosexuality per se. I, however, disagree with the view. If human sexuality exists on a six-point scale, the vast majority of human beings, as explained earlier, *must* have a homosexual side to them, which may remain dormant all their lives. Situations, however, may serve as a catalyst that enables them to recognize and acknowledge this side. Thus, to suggest that situational homosexuality is unnatural is misleading. In an intertitle inserted between two vignettes in his experimental film *BomGay* (1996), the late Riyad Wadia, quoting a government agency, goes to the extent of suggesting that 50 million Indian men have, at some point in their lives, had sex with other men.

To MSMs, unlike other queers, the active/passive dichotomy is a crucial factor in same-sex sexual activity. As stated in Chapter I, both in casual sexual encounters as well as in relationships, MSMs project themselves as penetrators. The fact that they are usually not effeminate or camp, and that most of them are married men, nourishes the stereotype. In their scheme of things, a strict division exists in their anatomies between male and female body parts. Thus, while the penis and testicles are male, the anus and nipples are female. In sexual activity with men, MSMs often recoil at the touch of their 'female' body parts, for this to them may be indicative of the fact that their partners view them not as men, but as women. It may also seem like a prelude to their being penetrated by their partners, which can set alarm bells ringing. Real homophobia probably does not exist in Hindu India's shame culture as opposed to the guilt culture of the Christian West (see Chapter V). However, regardless of what their fantasies and fetishes might in truth be, the blow suffered by their masculinized notion of self at being penetrated, or even touched in the 'female' zones, can provoke MSMs into homophobic violence. The violence could take manifold forms such as gay bashing, blackmail, extortion, and so on. Riyad Wadia believed that MSMs did not suffer from a gender identity crisis and were unable to distinguish between men and women during penetrative sexual activity. In other words, as long as they were penetrators, it mattered little whether who they fucked was a man or a woman.

Several interviews conducted by my co-editor and I in *Whistling in the Dark* bear testimony to this. For example, Satish Ranadive, now a married MSM with children, says:

> I believe in strict gender roles. Nature made man to be the penetrator and that's how it should be. Without this, how can the life cycle continue? I may be homosexually inclined, but I'm still a man. I'll never agree that I'm a *koti* [an effeminate gay man who is usually passive in the sex act] even if you convince me that my body language is that of a *koti*.
>
> (Rao and Sarma, 2009: 67)

Another respondent, Aslam Shaikh, an auto-rickshaw driver by profession who is also married with kids, when probed about charging for sex said:

> Women are commodities, not men. I don't know what you mean by male prostitution…. Okay, so I have had sex with men, but that's different. That wasn't my job. I did it for the heck of it. If women are not available, any man turns to other men. But we don't talk about it the way we talk about our encounters with women, or even boast about them. If we did, the person opposite will think we're mad and should get our heads checked.
>
> (Rao and Sarma, 2009: 124)

In this way, Shaikh cleverly skirts the issue of male prostitution. Also, his tendency to pluralize and universalize, and speak not merely in terms of his own experiences, but about men as a class, needs to be especially taken into account.

The perceptions of MSMs as free men in a heteropatriarchal culture (in Foucault's sense) cannot be overstated. But this, despite the inherent queerness prevalent in any same-sex sexual activity, makes them essentialist rather than transgressive.

Andre Gide saw succumbing to homosexual desire as temptation that invariably led to sin. Gide saw homosexual desire as a sin because sex, as the Bible taught, was something that happened between a man and a woman. If this belief contradicted Gide's own chromosomal nature (Sedgwick, 1990: 27), his impulse would be to abstain from sexual activity altogether, except when tempted by transgressors like Oscar Wilde.

Gide's steadfast faith in religion may find a parallel in the steadfast faith of modern MSMs in gender, the Hindu idea of Ardhanarishvara notwithstanding. If, to Gide, his Protestantism taught him that sexual activity legitimately took place between a man and a woman, the blind adherence to gender and the inability to see it as "performativity" (Butler, 1990: 25) causes modern MSMs to see the penis as a penetrative organ—nothing less, nothing more. In this way, MSMs essentialize the body.

Such essentialism, rather than destabilizing normativity, pushes MSMs in the direction of normativity. The homosexual side of their nature, which has the inbuilt potential to dismantle the hetero/homo binary and go beyond it, keeps it instead in place. MSMs, therefore, are far from transgressive or radical. On the contrary, they may be described as orthodox, conservative, and status quoist. To Oscar Wilde, transgression was the key to utopia.

Oscar Wilde's transgressive paradigm did not merely con-done homosexuality. Instead, it "authorized evil" (Dollimore, 1991: 5). It also dismissed "the related pieties, that humankind learns wisdom through suffering, and that suffering humanizes" (Dollimore, 1991: 7). To Wilde, individualism and socialism were the means to decenter conformity. The obvious lack of individualism and socialism in the familial culture of post-global India guarantees conformism on the part of MSMs. Few same-sex identities in the country, then, such as transgender and hijra identities, emerge as truly queer. An understanding of how these identities differ radically from MSM identities is, in the view of this researcher, best provided by the following paragraph, quoted in full, in an essay entitled "Us 'Sexuality Types'" by Akshay Khanna (the author's name, too, parodies an identical name of a macho Bollywood star):

> I look apparently male, have long hair tied into a bun, wear nail polish, bangles and hand-me-downs (largely) from wardrobes of my women

friends. I have pretensions of challenging ideas of masculinity, of the male–female dualism of 'natural' genders and heteronormativity. I have been often asked whether I am 'ladies or gents', sometimes in a friendly way, sometimes in an aggressive manner. At the same time, my class is written on my body, my language and my attire. Had I been from a lower economic strata, I would perhaps have been identified as a hijra. It seems that this confusion of colours and class does not always make sense. It raises eyebrows, attracts all the attention one can ever want on the street, whispers, giggles and sometimes, unfortunately, aggression. In touristic places where, perhaps the easier way to make sense of my gender performance (and my visible class) is by considering me a 'foreigner', people almost always initiate a conversation with me in English. In the UK, where I *am* a 'foreigner', I am just another South Asian man with long hair.... Although I do not, here, intend to examine in detail these different ways in which visible performances of gender are interpreted, I do wish to highlight that these experiences suggest that 'gender' is contextual and that its functioning is enmeshed in local discourses of normality, otherness, nationalism, class etc.

(Bose and Bhattacharyya, 2007: 161–162)

Transgression, to Oscar Wilde, implied "a radical possibility of freedom 'latent and potential in mankind generally'" (Dollimore, 1991: 8). Utopia is achieved through disobedience and rebellion, whereas uniformity of type and conformity to rule are attributed by him to class and ruling ideologies. Dollimore concludes:

Even nature, conceived as the opposite of culture and art, retains a social dimension...especially when it signifies nature as ideological mystification of the social; that is why, for [Oscar] Wilde, anyone trying to be natural is posing, and embarrassingly so, since they are trying to mystify the social as natural.

(Dollimore, 1991: 10)

While not actively lending support to the pro-gay marriage lobby in India and elsewhere in the world on account of the denial they are in, MSMs tacitly endorse the idea of husbands and wives in same-sex relationships. The fact that they are themselves married, and that the birth of biological children has consummated their marriages, prompts them to see

themselves as husbands. But the same-sex partners they seek
out, who frequently are unmarried men, *kotis* perhaps, are
not *also* seen as husbands but as 'wives'. The heteronormative
paradigm is thus replicated here, with all its attendant ills
of gender discrimination. Potentially, the effeminate male
partner, then, could be the one who does not go to work to
earn a living, but stays home to do the cooking and washing.
In some cases, the effeminate male could also become a
victim of gay bashing by his MSM partner, which may be seen
as the equivalent of wife-beating in a heterosexual alliance.
The specter of MSMs in India having hijras and transsexuals
as partners also cannot be ruled out, as Pooja Bhatt's 1990s
film *Tamanna* shows. The masculinity of the MSM, then, is
preserved; it remains intact. The MSM man's identification,
obviously, is with heterosexual men rather than with queers.
At best, the MSM man may be said to homonormativize the
heteronormative. The term 'homonormativity' was first used
by the queer theorist Lisa Duggan. She defines it as "A politics
that does not contest dominant heteronormative assumptions
and institutions, but upholds and sustains them" (Duggan,
2003: 54). Jack Halberstam has also written on the subject
of homonormativity (2011).

In conclusion, one may say that MSMs neither invert the
hetero/homo binary as required by gay theory, nor go beyond
it as queer theory advocates. Unlike race, class, caste, and
gender, sexuality for MSMs does not constitute an axis on
which their identity can be plotted. In fact, MSMs pooh-pooh
the idea that sexuality can be anything but the gratification of
desire. Their attitude to sex is typified by a remark made by an
upper middle-class lesbian contributor, Rita, in the anthology
Facing the Mirror, who writes, "I just want to *be* gay; I don't
want to attend conferences about it" (Sukthankar, 1999: xxix).
To the extent MSMs are in the closet, they may be said to use
the trope of homosociality as an alibi to conceal their same-
sex activity. Thus, when seen in the company of other men,

the association would pass for friendship, though in truth it is sexual. Ironically, the refusal of MSMs to see sexuality as a determinant of identity has boomeranged in a post-AIDS scenario, where support groups in India include them in their classification of alternative sexualities, especially on account of their potential to transmit the HIV virus, not just to other men but also to wives and unborn children. In fact, one reason why a petition filed by one such support group (The Naz Foundation) reached the Delhi High Court and eventually the Supreme Court of India is that the Indian Health Ministry saw merit in the arguments of the said support group. It differed with the views of the Indian home ministry, which categorically ruled that homosexuality was against Indian culture and was a Western import not indigenous to the culture of India.

At the beginning of the 21st century, Ruth Vanita and Saleem Kidwai complained that while Indian academia was quick to jump on to the bandwagon of new-fangled ideas originating in the West, such as Marxism, feminism, postmodernism, and deconstruction, it backed off when it came to gay and lesbian studies. This, they implied, was because of the deep-seated conservatism of Indian society (Vanita and Kidwai, 2001: xiv). I would also attribute it to hypocrisy. However, in the humanities and liberal arts, with topics such as postcolonialism, women's studies, and Dalit studies having reached saturation point, researchers have had to parasitically and opportunistically turn to queer studies for succor. This has made it possible for sexuality to be included as a category in discussions on identity.

Still, if we define identity politics in India as that which exists on the axes of caste, gender, and sexuality, the first two categories do not face the hostility that the third category does. In the case of gender, though it has to do with sex since in most cases it is one's sex that determines one's gender, we foreground the social construction of gender when we talk about it, rather than the fact that all females have a vagina. However, there is no social construction of sexuality. One can speak of a woman as a wife, but one can only speak of a homosexual man as being active or passive in bed. Thus, while caste and gender can be easily politicized, the politicization of sexuality is fraught with difficulty. Even the vocabulary is opposed to it. There is no such word as 'homopolitical' in English, though some queer activists speak of 'homonationalism' (Ghosh, 2015: 176). The lesbians only have it slightly better, with lesbianism, after all, being an 'ism' such as Marxism and feminism. There is also the aspect of political lesbianism (see Chapter VI).

Deviant sexuality marginalizes those in possession of it as much as other identity markers on the axes of caste, class, race, and gender. Yet, the oppressor–victim binary is not universally applied to homosexuals. Ironically, a homosexual does not wear his sexuality on his sleeve. One can differentiate between a man and woman, or upper and lower class, or black and white people on the basis of external appearance. Not so in the case of homosexuals, because of deep-seated heterosexism that assumes heterosexuality to be universal. In other words, how can we tell a gay man on the street? To speak about gender, no one can deny that women are oppressed in Indian society. Yet, rape laws, as we know, have recently been amended to the advantage of women. Then there are other pro-women laws, such as the anti-dowry law and amniocentesis law.

In his book *Courting Injustice*, author Rajesh Talwar discusses how the new rape laws, which came into effect after the Nirbhaya rape case of December 2012, actually discriminate against men and boys. If a minor boy is sexually assaulted by a man, the latter cannot be charged under the IPC. He can only be charged under an act known as the Prevention of Children from Sexual Offences (POCSO) Act. On the other hand, a man who sexually assaults a minor girl can be tried under both the POCSO Act as well as the IPC. Talwar points out that "there have been frequent reports over the years of objects being inserted into the rectums of male prisoners in holding cells and police stations, with a view to forcing them to confess their crimes" (Talwar, 2008: 35). Yet these acts do not come within the definition of rape because the victim is a male. By contrast, when it comes to women, Talwar informs us that the definition of rape has been expanded to include not just penetration but other forms of forced sexual contact as well. He laments the fact that the new rape laws only protect women from sexual assault and rape, and not men and transgendered people. Talwar thus calls the new rape laws "discriminatory." He argues that if the new rape laws were gender-neutral, providing for the rape of both men and women, they would have served to put an end to the torture of men in police stations and other custodial situations.

Why does this anomaly in the law exist? It exists because the framers of the law see heterosexuality as natural and homosexuality as unnatural. But then, does not this shockingly imply that heterosexual rape, though a crime, is nevertheless natural, whereas homosexual rape is unnatural?

Talwar, as stated earlier, calls the new rape laws discriminatory. To me, they are also discriminatory in the matter of consent. A straight man may be acquitted of the charge of rape if he can prove that the sex was consensual. A gay or transgendered man cannot be similarly acquitted, even if he proves that the sex was consensual, because the Supreme Court judgment of December 2013 implies that mere consent cannot de-criminalize a homosexual (and therefore criminal) act.

Nivedita Menon, in a well-known essay titled "Would YOU Pass a Gender Test?" (Ghosh, 2015: 149–167), says that three sets of characteristics determine sexual identity. The first is genetic (the XX female and XY male chromosomal pattern). The second is hormonal (estrogen, female; androgen/testosterone, male). The third is genital (female, vagina; male, penis). According to Menon, "...if a body has female genitals it is not necessarily the case that it would have preponderantly female chromosomes and female hormones. Moreover, sex chromosomes themselves often defy the pattern of XX (women) and XY (men)...."

Based on the earlier data, perhaps it is a fallacy to say that there are only two genders, male and female. There are, in fact, at least six genders that can be deduced. Moreover, no one can say with certainty that they are either male or female, though these are the boxes that society puts us into. Most people are surprised when they are told that there are at least six genders. 'Male' and 'female' are of course the two broad gender categories. But then, there are men who feel that they are really women and women who feel that they are really men. Such people are born male or female alright, but the biological gender they are assigned at birth is in conflict with their psychological identity. We call such people 'transgender', this being the third gender after 'male' and 'female'. Many transgender people live with the duality all their life. Some, however, act upon it and have sex reassignment (or realignment) surgery. Put simply, this is a sex-change operation that enables a man to become a woman and a woman to become a man. A man who has a sex-change operation and becomes a woman is known as a trans-woman. Likewise, a woman who has a sex-change operation and becomes a man is known as a trans-man. These, then, are two other genders, distinct from the first three genders stated earlier, bringing the total to five. In India, most hijras are also trans-women (see further). The sixth gender category is what we call 'intersex'. Intersex people are sometimes called 'hermaphrodite'. They are born with ambiguous genitalia, making it difficult to determine if they are male or female. National Geographic Channel once featured an intersex person who had both breasts and a penis.

Gender categories other than male and female lead stigmatized lives. Society expects human beings to be either male or female, and deviation from the norm is viewed with prejudice. Thus, many trans-men do not want it to be known that they were born female, and many trans-women do not want it to be known that they were born male. It is presumptuous on the part of human beings to define themselves as either men or women, because there are all the other genders to contend with. One may be a male and yet not a man. One may be female and yet not a woman. The social and psychological construction of gender is different from its biological construction.

While the hijras in India may be regarded as trans-women, many of them retain their male genitalia and are thus not trans-women in the true sense. Hijras do not have sex-change operations. They have castration rites known as their *nirvana*. Hijras are more transparent as compared to trans-men and trans-women. We know that they were 'male' to start with, and are now hijras. There are well-known hijras in India. Two of them, Laxmi and Revathi, have written their autobiographies (Tripathi, 2015; Revathi, 2010). Another hijra, Nisha, features in the YouTube series Project Bolo (2012), directed by Sridhar Rangayan. Laxmi, Revathi, and Nisha, together with Famila, an educated hijra who committed suicide, defy our stereotypes about hijras. We think of hijras as beggars, mascots, and sex workers. But the life stories of Laxmi, Revathi, Nisha, and Famila give us a very different picture of hijra life. These hijras overcame their victimhood through education and activism, and became a source of inspiration to other hijras. Yet, hijras are lonely and alone. Their families abandon them. In patriarchal cultures like ours, where the desire to have sons is so over-abiding, that doctors will perform illegal ultrasound tests on mothers to determine a fetus' gender, the thought of a son voluntarily becoming a hijra is bewildering to parents. They are overcome by shame. Hijras thus have no option but to leave the house and join hijra *gharana*s, each with its own *naik*s, gurus, and *chela*s.

The lesbian anthology *Facing the Mirror* has a subversive story titled "The Complete Works of Someshwar P. Balendu" by a trans-man who suffocates in her female body and wants to get rid of it as soon as she can (Sukthankar, 1999: 267–286). The narrator is Purnima, who acquired this name because the family pundit told her mother that her name should begin with the letter P. When Purnima grew up, this same pundit told her mother to take her to a doctor as there was something wrong with her. This was because Purnima was tomboyish and a chain-smoker; she sported a boy cut and used street slang. In reply, Purnima asked her mother to feed the pundit "the leg of a tandoori chicken as Prasad," and wipe her greasy fingers on his dhoti. Purnima frustrated all her mother's attempts to feminize her by deciding to have her breasts removed in the general ward of a municipal hospital. The surgery was excruciatingly painful, despite the anesthesia and the painkillers and sedatives that the nurses gave her. After the surgery, Purnima was wrapped in bandages which became "stiff as a Kurukshetra warrior's shield." But she was filled with such destructive tendencies as she lay in her hospital bed that she wanted to rip off her bandages in a fit of rage. Idly, Purnima wondered what the hospital authorities would do with her severed breasts. She wrote, "I was not sure but I thought my breasts might have been thrown into the municipal dustbin, buried in mango peels, eggshells, tea leaves, and crusted sanitary napkins until dogs or a sweeper's broom found them, ripening in the heat." When Purnima asked the nurse what they would do with her breasts, the latter sarcastically remarked, "This is a charity hospital. We don't have incinerators; we throw away lungs, brains, livers, umbilical cords. What do you expect us to do—make pickles?" Purnima's surgery successfully transformed her into a man. She became a trans-man. She left her mother's home and began to live by herself in a rented room. She switched to male attire, wearing shirts with stiff collars and trousers with metal buttons. She felt like a "prince in the crowds." An Afghan hawker, seeing her as a man, sold her herbs that would increase her *mardaangi*. He said, "*Beta*, I promise you'll be on top of her so often and for so long, you'll scrape the skin off your knees." Purnima was not Purnima anymore. She was Someshwar P. Balendu. As she walked through the streets, she spotted a roadside stall selling brassieres. The sight of the brassieres sickened her so much that she wanted to throw up.

Zaid Al Baset, in an essay titled "The Fiction(s) of Identity" (Ghosh, 2015: 168–175), presents the case history of Subhankar, who, to put it reductively, is a trans-woman, though he has his penis. Subhankar claims that there are both a woman and a man within him, the woman being "heterosexual" as well as the man's "alter ego." Subhankar says that when 'he' has anonymous sex with a man, it is 'he' and not 'his' alter ego who is performing the act. But when 'he' has sex with a man 'he' loves, it is 'his' alter ego, the straight woman, who is performing the act. Subhankar's sex acts, of course, whether it is 'he' or 'his' alter ego who is performing them, are passive or bottom sex acts where he is penetrated by 'his' male partner anally, without 'him' having an erection. Al Baset thus calls Subhankar's case "a queer case par excellence." According to her:

> Subhankar...is an impossible subject to signify in two senses: (a) his self minus the 'alter ego' is a non 'he' and not 'her'; (b) his alter ego is a 'her' who is not really a woman because 'he' has a penis and to that extent 'she' is not really a woman.

The only conclusion that Al Baset can come to is that Subhankar is a "fictive" person. She says:

> In this miasma of 'man'/'woman', 'masculine'/'feminine', 'him'/'her', 'he'/'she', Subhankar's identity, his 'self' is difficult to write; his 'self' translated in writing transforms 'him' by imposing a syntax of gender that fails to signify him.... On [the] page Subhankar 'becomes' a fiction.

Subhankar reminds us of Terry Goldie, who says that "my preferred form of sex is anal, with me as the receiver of my partner's penis." Yet, unlike Subhankar who speaks of a female alter ego, Goldie perceives himself as "overtly male" during sex. He defends his position (pun unintended) in the following words: "If the male desire to insert is simply to achieve orgasm, then...I have the most powerful orgasm when masturbating with a penis in my anus" (Goldie, 2008: 120).

Goldie's gender identity, then, unlike Subhankar's, is not, in Al Baset's formulation, 'fictive'.

Eve Sedgwick elaborately discusses the complex relationship between gender and sexuality in *Axiom 2* of her book *Epistemology of the Closet* (Sedgwick, 1990: 27–35). The axiom reads, "The study of sexuality is not coextensive with the study of gender; correspondingly, antihomophobic inquiry is not coextensive with feminist inquiry. But we can't know in advance how they will be different." To Sedgwick, sex is chromosomal, whereas gender is social. However, sex is the "raw material" on which gender is based. Thus, "Gender...is the far more elaborated, more fully and rigidly dichotomized social production and reproduction of male and female identities and behaviors...." This implies that while sex is immutable and immanent in the individual, gender is culturally mutable and variable. Gender is also relational in that each gender is defined in terms of its relation to the other gender(s). In support of her contention, Sedgwick quotes from an essay titled "Thinking Sex" by Gayle Rubin, who writes:

> I want to challenge the assumption that feminism is or should be the privileged site of a theory of sexuality. Feminism is the theory of gender oppression.... Gender affects the operation of the sexual system, and the sexual system has had gender-specific manifestations. But although sex and gender are related, they are not the same thing.

Sedgwick concedes that without a concept of gender there cannot be a concept of homosexuality and heterosexuality. However, she argues that it is fallacious to speak of sexual object choice merely in terms of gender. That is to say, a homosexual's preference cannot merely be defined in terms of his sexual attraction to people of his own gender. It would exist on other dimensions as well, that bear no connection to gender. For example, a gay man may prefer alloeroticism to autoeroticism. He may prefer interracial and intergenerational sex to sex with people of his own race and generation. Belonging to the middle class, he may prefer to have sex with people of the working class. And so on. The tendency to prioritize gender in discussions of sexual preference is, according to Sedgwick, a mistake.

In respect of identity, the axis of gender came before the axis of sexuality. Thus, Sedgwick believes that "gay/lesbian and antihomophobic inquiry still has a lot to learn from asking questions that feminist inquiry has learned to ask...." One of the questions that feminist inquiry is routinely concerned with is how forms of oppression "intertwine" with each other, and cancel each other out. Sedgwick is especially concerned here with "how [a] person who is disabled through one set of oppressions may *by the same positioning* be enabled through others" (emphasis original). To illustrate her point, Sedgwick provides us with two examples. First, the understated demeanor of educated women in our society tends to mark both their deference to educated men and their expectation of deference from women and men of lower class. Second, a woman's use of a married name makes graphic at the same time her subordination as a woman and her privilege as a presumptive heterosexual. In the first example, the educated woman is on the empowered side of the binary as far as class is concerned, but on its disempowered side in relation to gender. Likewise, in the second example, the woman is on the empowered side of the binary as far as sexuality is concerned, for as a married woman, she is presumably heterosexual; however, she is on the disempowered side of the binary as far as gender is concerned, because a married man's name and title do not reveal his marital status. Sedgwick provides a third example, concerning race. She says, "The distinctive vulnerability to rape women of all races has become...a powerful tool for racist enforcement by which white people, including women, are privileged at the expense of Black people of both genders." Sedgwick concludes:

That one is *either* oppressed or an oppressor, or that if one happens to be both, the two are not likely to have much to do with each other, still seems to be a common assumption...in...male gay writing and activism, as it hasn't for a long time been in careful feminist work.

III

Normativities

Why did Andre Gide avoid Oscar Wilde in Algeria? The reason was that he did not wish Wilde's path to cross his. Oscar Wilde was homosexual and so was Gide. Gide avoided Wilde because their approach to homosexuality was different. Gide was a devout Protestant to whom sexuality was subsumed by religion. Gide had come to terms with his sexuality no doubt, but felt that it called upon him to create a new integral self in place of an existing one, where nothing other than sexual object choice was different. If an oppositional desire (in terms of gender) led to heteronormativity, then Gide's conception of desire within the framework of Christianity took him in the direction of homonormativity. This is exactly what Oscar Wilde was opposed to. To Wilde, the belief that homosexuality was the handiwork of the Devil needed to be foregrounded. If homosexuality was a sin and a perversion (as the Bible called it), it had to be worn on one's sleeve rather than guiltily shunned. In other words, the homosexual had to be proud of the fact that he was a pervert. To Wilde, homosexuality was a transgression, nothing less, nothing more, and on this was founded his very aesthetic as a man of letters. In spite of Gide's attempts to avoid Wilde in Algeria, they finally met. Wilde introduced Gide to a dark-skinned flute player named

Mohammed, whom both of them were attracted to. Gide spent the night with Mohammed in a state of bliss and ecstasy, and came to the same conclusion that E. M. Forster later would in India—homosexuality was 'normal' and 'natural' for him. But the conclusion, to Wilde, was an essentialist conclusion that led to "uniformity of type" and "conformity to rule." On the other hand, Wilde believed in anti-essentialism and individualism in art and life that served to destabilize a conservative social order. Dollimore summarizes this difference of perception of the two men in the following words:

> For Gide, transgression is in the name of a desire and identity rooted in the natural, the sincere, the authentic. Wilde's transgressive aesthetic is the reverse: insincerity, inauthenticity and unnaturalness become the liberating attributes of decentred identity and desire, and inversion becomes central to Wilde's expression of this aesthetic....
>
> (Dollimore, 1991: 14)

To Gide's way of thinking, Wilde's formulation was not just subversive; it was downright selfish because it did not take the moral values of civil society (in today's terms) into account. Hence, in the letter to his mother, Gide described Wilde as "a most dangerous product of modern civilization" (Dollimore, 1991: 5). However, as Dollimore says, to Wilde, selfishness consisted not in living as one desired to, but in asking others to live as one desired to. To 'demoralize', then, meant to liberate the soul from moral constraint.

As pointed out in Chapter I, to Foucault, the homosexuality of the ancient Greeks and Romans was no homosexuality. Instead, it was sodomy. While the former term implies gender transitivity, where the homosexual man may be both the penetrator and the penetrated (i.e., both active and passive in bed), the latter term implies gender intransitivity, where the sodomite is merely the penetrator. The penetrated, by this formulation, was not a man but a slave. He was usually a beardless boy (as opposed to a bearded man), and was consigned to play the passive role in bed. In Foucault's words, "To be fucked is a necessity for a slave, a shame for a free man, and a favor returned for an emancipated slave." Foucault frequently reiterates that "it is immoral for a free young man to be fucked" (Lotringer, 1996: 364).

If Oscar Wilde's anti-essentialist theories of perversion and transgression are applied to Foucault's slave, we see at once, as explained earlier, that ironically it is the slave rather than the free man who is given the onerous task of toppling a conservative social order and destabilizing normativity. The free man, then, emerges as not substantially different from the patriarchal heterosexual man. Foucault himself refers to the "return of monosexuality" where there is "a very clear separation between men and women" (Lotringer, 1996: 367). The average homosexual of today is the sodomite of yesterday who, as stated earlier, has passed through the three stages of persecution—by the Church, the law, and the medical fraternity respectively.

Foucault, quoted in Chapter I, intriguingly says, "To be gay is to be in a state of becoming…. It is not necessary to be homosexual, but it is necessary to be set on being gay" (Lotringer, 1996: 370).

What does Foucault mean by the statement? To start with, Foucault is making a distinction between the words 'homosexual' and 'gay' which we tend to use synonymously today. He says, "Not to be gay is to say: 'How am I going to be able to limit the effects of my sexual choice in such a way that my life *doesn't* change (my emphasis) in any way?'" (Lotringer, 1996: 370) The question has to do with lifestyle choices, and it brings Foucault remarkably close to the views expressed by Oscar Wilde in the previous century. Foucault is here suggesting that if one is in possession of a 'deviant' sexuality, one must use it to radicalize one's ways of seeing. Such a radicalization would, for one, have to do with an inversion of received notions of morality that condemn all forms of sex other than monogamous vaginal sex between husband and wife for the purpose of procreation. There are a plethora of sexual behaviors and practices that Foucault's position would validate, and these would include adultery, incest, bestiality, pedophilia, cunnilingus, and fellatio, none of which can lead to the birth of 'legitimate' offspring (see Chapter VII). But rather than call them sexual behaviors or sexual practices, Foucault would call them "sexual choices" that are conducive to creative ways of living. Thus, Oscar Wilde's transgressive aesthetic and Foucault's distinction between being homosexual and being set on being gay are both concerned with the destabilizing of normativity through the decentering of morality.

Terry Goldie, referred to in Chapter I, comes across as a faithful follower of Oscar Wilde and Michel Foucault. Goldie openly admits to being what he calls "anal passive" (Foucault's slave) without any traces of guilt and shame, which implies, for one thing, that he has demolished for himself all received notions of sociality and morality. But Goldie is anything but homonormative. Confessing that he was born to be a parent, the book provides a photograph of him with his two latest babies on the last page. Incidentally, Goldie has had several other babies in the past, some of whom are now way into their thirties. This leads Goldie to point out that "receptive anal sex for me is not limited to homosexuality." In this context, he further explains that on occasion "I have had women use strap-ons and I have used a double-ended dildo, with one end in the woman's vagina and the other in my anus" (Goldie, 2008: 125). In a way, Goldie, in the manner of Roland Barthes, rejects the active/passive binary and attempts to get beyond it. If anal sex implies passivity and gender intransitivity, Goldie says that although he has never himself indulged in active sex, that is, penetrated a man or woman with his penis, he is "overtly male" in another sense. He then goes on to explain what he means: "If the male desire to insert is simply to achieve orgasm, then that would reflect my choice: I have the most powerful orgasm when masturbating with a penis in my anus" (Goldie, 2008: 120).

Elsewhere in the chapter, Goldie talks about fantasy, "...I must admit a flirtation with the transsexual when being fucked by a man. I find that when I am being penetrated by a penis, I sometimes fantasize about being penetrated vaginally" (Goldie, 2008: 129).

The explicit vocabulary that Goldie employs in his book (as the aforequoted statements testify) subverts the very language of scholarship and verges on the pornographic. But that is what Wilde probably meant by a transgressive aesthetic, restricted to not just subject matter but inclusive of form, and to not just literature but inclusive of criticism. *Queersexlife* certainly invites us to defer our judgment on the value of the book, for we have nothing quite like it anywhere in the world.

Eve Sedgwick's *Epistemology of the Closet*, while deploying an alternative set of terminologies, endorses Wilde's formulations of anti-essentialism and individualism. To Sedgwick, the polarization is between a "minoritizing" and a "universalizing" or "constructivist" view. Sedgwick defines a minoritizing view as one that sees "homo/heterosexual definition...as an issue of active importance primarily for a small, distinct, relatively fixed homosexual minority." On the other hand, she defines a universalizing or constructivist view as "an issue of continuing, determinative importance in the lives of people across the spectrum of sexualities" (Sedgwick, 1990: 1).

In the 20th and 21st centuries, the gay community worldwide has opted to refer to itself as a minority community, or a sexual minority, to be more exact. In Sedgwick's formulation,. this is a minoritizing view that can lead its proponents to the antithetical states of homonormativity and 'heterophobia', derived obviously from heteronormativity and homophobia. Sedgwick's own preference is for the constructivist view that takes into account a "spectrum of sexualities" that may be interpreted as not just lesbian, gay, bisexual, transgender, transsexual, intersexual, hijra, *koti*, etc., but, more significantly, as that which inherently has within itself an inbuilt resisting mechanism that protects it from normativity in general.

At the same time, Sedgwick's universalizing spectrum of sexualities is simultaneously resistant to the idea of continuums and coalitions. Thus, a feminist-lesbian continuum, as Sedgwick herself, as well as influential queer theorists such as Judith Butler and Gayle Rubin have eloquently and painstakingly pointed out, is a myth (Sedgwick, 1990: 36). As pointed out in Chapter I, in India, this was proved during the release of Deepa Mehta's *Fire* in 1998, when lesbians who joined the protests against the Shiv Sena's call to ban the film were accused of hijacking the protests (Sukthankar, 1999: Editor's Note), since the film, according to the heterosexual feminists who accused the lesbians, was not a lesbian film per se.

Again, a gay–lesbian continuum or coalition is a myth. This has been proved, among others, by Adrienne Rich in her famous essay "Compulsory Heterosexuality and Lesbian Existence." (Sedgwick, 1990: 36). Commenting on Rich's rich work, Eve Sedgwick writes:

> In so far as lesbian object choice was viewed as epitomizing a specificity of female experience and resistance, in so far as a symmetrically opposite understanding of gay male object choice also obtained, and in so far also as feminism necessarily posited male and female experiences and interests as different and opposed, the implication was that an understanding of male homo/heterosexual definition could offer little or no affordance of interest for any lesbian theoretical project.
>
> (Sedgwick, 1990: 37)

Similarly, in her essay "The Lesbian Standpoint" in *The Phobic and the Erotic: The Politics of Sexualities in Contemporary India* (Bose and Bhattacharyya, 2007: 263–290), Ranjita Biswas suggests that lesbians, who generally uphold feminist arguments against patriarchy, come into conflict with gay men who interpret Foucault's advocacy of lifestyle change as a carte blanche for promiscuity, which among other things has led to the AIDS epidemic of the 20th century. Continuums and coalitions by this formulation come across as essentialist, rather than as constructivist and individualist.

In my own case, my life and my work have been a continuous exploration of and experiment with the destabilizing of normativity. My protagonists and I may be described as autoerotic rather than alloerotic, and gender intransitive rather than gender transitive, in terms of sexual behavior and identity. In *The Boyfriend* (Rao, 2003), Yudi invokes Aristotle to explain why masturbation to him is superior to alloerotic sex: a masturbation fantasy belongs to the realm of representation that is a heightened version of reality. It is like the painter's bed (in Aristotle's formulation) as opposed to the carpenter's bed. It thus exemplifies Oscar Wile's transgressive aesthetic.

Ageist and classist sexual criteria recur in my life and work. In *BomGay* (Rao, 2006), *The Boyfriend*, and other fictions and poems, the sexual object choice is always a man from the lower or working class (the great Indian underclass), much younger in age than the protagonist who is from the bourgeois middle class. In *The Boyfriend*, Yudi contrasts his relationship to Milind with a typical heteronormative relationship by pointing out that what must be same/similar (age, class) is different in their case, and what must be different (gender) is same in their case.

In both my life and work, my protagonists, though straight-acting and not camp, are Foucault's slaves rather than Foucault's free men, who, like Terry Goldie, are gender intransitive and passive in the sex act. This voluntary embracing of sexual slavery and servitude may be a means of dismantling an oppressive moral and socio-political order. However, it is also a means of cancelling out a seeming class privilege that the bourgeois male protagonists in my life and work possess. This is an issue that Pramod K. Nayar overlooks in his essay "Queering Culture Studies: Notes towards a Framework" in *The Phobic and the Erotic* (Bose and Bhattacharyya, 2007: 117–148), as he calls Yudi's relationship with Milind in *The Boyfriend* 'exploitative' (presumably in the Marxist sense). But Ruth Vanita in her book

Love's Rite: Same Sex Marriage in India and the West (Vanita, 2005: 244) explains how Yudi's seeming class privilege is neutralized in another sense: as the man who chooses not to marry on account of his gayness, it is he who remains excluded, as compared to the bisexual Milind who eventually gets married and becomes a part of mainstream heteronormative society.

As pointed out earlier, Foucault speaks of 'monosexual society' where there is "a very clear separation between men and women" (Lotringer, 1996: 364). Doubtless, such monosexual communities existed in ancient Greece and Rome, but they also exist in Islamic society, with its insistence on *purdah*, as well as in Hindu, Buddhist, and Christian monasteries. Then, the kind of segregation of the genders that one finds in prisons, dorms, the armed forces, and so on may also amount to living in a monosexual society. What Foucault is really concerned with, however, is how a simple inversion of the hetero/homo binary, without any attempt to deconstruct it, fosters monosexuality. He says, "Thus, that you have homosexuals who live in a group or community, in a relation of constant exchange, reveals completely the return of monosexuality" (Lotringer, 1996: 365).

Monosexuality is essentialist by definition. The fact that it is practiced in monasteries, nunneries, the state-run armed forces, educational institutions, and so on also makes it right wing. As stated earlier, in my Introduction to *Whistling in the Dark: Twenty-one Queer Interviews*, I identify several monosexual, or non-heteronormative male single-sex spaces as I call them, in contemporary Indian towns and cities. These are the *nukkad* or street corner, the public urinal, the beer and country liquor bar, the *paan–beedi* and *gutkha* stall, the gents' hair cutting saloon, the auto-rickshaw stand, the second-class local train compartment, and so on In these spaces, mischief rules, the watchword is *masti*, and the idiom macho (Rao and Sarma, 2009: xx–xxi). Thus, in the incident that took place in a Mangalore pub some time ago, where women drinking in the pub were assaulted by men in the name of morality, my take on the episode is that the men were really threatened by an invasion of monosexual space by the women.

Foucault critiques monosexuality in the context of homosexuals living in a group or community. I would take his use of the words 'group' and 'community' to refer specifically to the gay support groups and gay community of the West, post-Stonewall, and, by extension, those, say, of India, post-globalization. These communities perpetuate the idea of normativity by substituting homonormativity for heteronormativity, and, correspondingly, 'heterophobia' and misogyny for homophobia. Normativity of any type does nothing to dismantle the status quo; it is only through a destabilizing of normativity that revolutionary change can occur. Thus, we must oppose the idea of Gay Pride and gay marriage. Or, to reiterate, normativity engenders essentialism.

Foucault speaks of his native France. Here two institutions in particular come in for sharp criticism—the law and medicine. Speaking of the law, he says, "A whole system of traps and threats is set up, with cops and police spies, a little world is put into place very early, in the 17th and 18th centuries" (Lotringer, 1996: 369).

In contemporary India, the public face of Section 377 of the IPC (see Chapter IX) has been those very traps, threats, cops, and police spies that Foucault refers to in the context of Europe. When the petition for the revoking or reading down of Section 377 was being heard in the Supreme Court, an observation made by the Government of India was that very few actual convictions had taken place under Section 377. The reason? Money changed hands at the constabulary level; policemen set up traps and served as spies and agent provocateurs in mufti at places such as public parks and public urinals, where homosexuals networked. These *havildars*, once their palms were greased, were happy and contented, and did not let the matter (of the networking) reach the courts.

Foucault says, "This is all inscribed within the framework of a surveillance and organization of a world of prostitutes—kept women, dancers, actresses—fully developing in the 18th century." In this context, one may speak of the ban imposed on bar girls by the Maharashtra government a few years ago, which continues to be in place even today, despite a Bombay High Court order to the contrary.

Coming to medicine, Foucault speaks of the "noisy entry of homosexuality into the field of medical reflection in the mid-19th century" (Lotringer, 1996: 369). Noisy, probably, because medicine pathologizes homosexuality more vociferously than either religious or legal texts. In America, as stated in Chapter I, where the American Psychiatric Association was obliged to strike homosexuality off its list of mental ailments, AIDS nevertheless caused heterosexist society as well as orthodox feminists to denounce the gay community. Attempts to resist the noisy entry of homosexuality into the field of medical reflection have been made, I think, by the anti-AIDS lobby and their conspiracy theory. This lobby strongly believes that AIDS is a myth, foisted on the world by multinational drug cartels.

The most central view that Foucault expresses in his interview that needs to be elaborated concerns lifestyle. His intriguing statement here is, "...it is not necessary to be homosexual, but it is necessary to be set on being gay" (Lotringer, 1996: 370). When probed as to the meaning of the statement, Foucault replied, "Saying 'one must be set on being gay' puts oneself in a dimension where the sexual choices that one makes are present and have their effects over the whole of our life" (Lotringer, 1996: 369). Then he added,

...sexual choices must at the same time be *creative* of ways of life (emphasis mine). To be gay means that these choices spread across a whole life; it's also a certain way of refusing *existing lifestyles*; making sexual choice the *operator* of a change of existence.

(emphasis mine)

The operative words and phrases in the sentences quoted earlier are: (1) sexual choices, (2) creative, (3) existing lifestyles, and (4) change of existence. Let me take these up one by one.

1. Sexual choice implies that there is a spectrum of sexualities (Sedgwick) from which one can/must choose. For Sedgwick, the term 'sexuality' really means a range of sexual behaviors and practices, and by this formulation, most sexualities, apart from procreative heterosexual sexuality, are non-normative. Foucault's emphasis on sexual choice, then, must be taken to mean his upholding of a wide variety of non-normative sexualities.

2. If non-normative sexualities are also transgressive sexualities (Dollimore), Foucault sees transgression as creative (artistic, aesthetic) and perversion as power. This is perhaps best understood in terms of Dollimore's Nature/Culture binary, where attributes in the X Column (Culture) must be substituted for attributes in the Y Column (Nature). These are as follows:

X	for	Y
surface		depth
lying		truth
change		stasis
difference		essence
persona/role		essential self
abnormal		normal
insincerity		sincerity
style/artifice		authenticity
facetious		serious
narcissism		maturity

(Dollimore, 1991: 10)

3. Existing lifestyles have to do with a maintenance of the status quo. They would make procreative (and hegemonic) heterosexual sex imperative in most cultures. Foucault

rejects existing sexual lifestyles, opting thereby for 'non-existent' ones, which would validate a whole host of 'outlawed' sexual behaviors and practices, including, to take the most outlawed ones, pedophilia, incest, bestiality, and S/M (Sado-masochism). (I have left out homosexuality and lesbianism from the list because these are already 'normative' and therefore 'existing' in many parts of the world). Ironically, it is the slave once again who becomes here the harbinger of change.

4. A change of existence is facilitated through (perverse) sexuality, making sexual choice the motor. The phrase 'change of existence' implies a dismantling of the status quo through a destabilizing of normativity. The formulation is 'militant' in import, for militants are said to destabilize the State.

Foucault finishes his reply to the question put to him by saying, "Not to be gay is to say: 'How am I going to be able to limit the effects of my sexual choice in such a way that my life *doesn't* change in any way?'" (Lotringer, 1996: 370; emphasis mine).

Two negatives make a positive; *limiting* sexual choice so that life does *not* change is tantamount to maintaining the status quo.

Therefore, "I would say that one must use sexuality to discover or invent new relations" (Lotringer, 1996: 370).

Foucault's "new relations" would even have to do with making 'relationships' out of outlawed sexual behaviors and practices, such as those mentioned earlier. In a Sappho for Equality seminar at Jadavpur University in September 2011, a participant spoke, for example, about a Calcutta sect that upheld and practiced S/M as a mode of sexual gratification. Other groups, such as the banned NAMBLA (North American Man Boy Love Association) similarly uphold and practice pedophilia. Incest and bestiality may also exist in random tribal and nontribal communities in different parts of the world.

Foucault finally says, "To be gay is to be in a state of becoming" (Lotringer, 1996: 370). This is because while 'being' is
essentialist, 'becoming' is anti-essentialist.

Foucault's views on sexuality are radical, and highlight the
difference between being gay, being homosexual, and being
queer. In post-Victorian India, few homosexual men and
almost no lesbians would be able to make the paradigm shift
from 'existing lifestyle' to 'change of existence'. The term 'community', as we have already seen, signifies 'existing lifestyle'.
Communities, thus, must be dissolved, whereas in India newer
and newer gay support groups, always monosexual, seem to be
emerging in metropolitan cities and smaller towns. The lesbian
predicament is best brought out by Ranjita Biswas. She writes:

> Staking claim to Foucault's theories of the sexual subject as a
> historical, cultural product, gay theorists have cast off their faith in
> the notion of a 'gay essence' and embarked on a detailed analysis
> of the historical construction of sexualities. This theoretical shift, as
> it were, finds realization in their personal lives too, as they portray
> a whole spectrum of sexually creative lifestyles and a proliferation
> of sexual cultures. Their supposed affinity for sexual pleasure as
> evident from their investment in anonymous lovers, pederasty, and
> their preoccupation with ageist standards of sexual attractiveness has
> drawn flak from lesbian activists and feminists alike.
>
> (Bose and Bhattacharyya, 2007: 278)

A justification for the rift is provided by Sedgwick in *Epistemology
of the Closet*, where Axiom 3 in the introductory chapter
"Axiomatic" reads as follows:

> There can't be an a priori decision about how far it will make sense to
> conceptualize lesbian and gay male identities together. Or separately.
>
> (Sedgwick, 1990: 36)

If Foucault's paradigm shift seems 'immoral' to some of us,
we must realize that it is *meant* to be so. Transgression and
perversion are to Foucault, as to Oscar Wilde and Jean Genet
before him, the route to utopia. That Foucault dreamt of utopia

is evident from his remark, "One day the question 'Are you homosexual?' will be as natural as the question 'Are you a bachelor?'" (Lotringer, 1996: 369).

Barthes also dreams of utopia when he says, "...once the paradigm is blurred, utopia begins: meaning and sex become the objects of free play, at the heart of which (polysemant) forms and the (sensual) practices, liberated from the binary prison, will achieve a state of infinite expansion" (Barthes, 1977: 133).

The binary, then, is a prison, and (sexual) practices must be sensual.

In 2014, the United Nations Human Rights Council (UNHRC) met to deliberate on the family. The United Nations has always viewed the family as a "natural and fundamental unit of society." The purpose of the meeting, however, was to examine if the definition of the term 'family' merited amendment in the 21st century. The family is not a monolith. The definition of the term 'family' is pluralistic, and varies from country to country, culture to culture. Socio-political factors such as forms of government and the fundamental rights of citizens, including those of women and children, play a crucial role in determining what constitutes the family. To the UNHRC, the family existed in "various forms," and these multiple forms of the institution had to be accorded recognition. Most countries that attended the meeting disagreed with the UNHRC premise. To these countries, the term 'family' meant that a man and a woman, united through marriage, biologically produced offspring, and the parents and their offspring taken together constituted the family. That this was a suspiciously Catholic Church kind of definition of the family did not bother the countries in question, several of which were not even Christian countries. In defining the family in this conventional way, they were putting undue emphasis on marriage, because marriage, by this formulation, was a precondition to the starting of a family. Led by Russia, these countries moved a No Action vote at the meeting, to stall discussion on the subject. Some of the countries that supported the No Action vote initiated by Russia were China, Uganda, Saudi Arabia, and India. Only two countries, France and Chile, disagreed with the No Action vote. These two countries wanted the conventional definition of family to be amended in order to recognize the diversity in the notion of the family. However, they being in the minority, their views could not be upheld.

Unfortunately, India sided with the group of countries that did not want the traditional definition of the family to be meddled with. There have always been multiple forms of family in India. There are joint and nuclear families. There are single-mother and single-father families. And there are families where the parents are not legally married, but are in a live-in relationship. In fact, in a recent judgment, the Supreme Court had even ruled that when a live-in relationship ended, the woman, if unemployed, was entitled to receive maintenance from her partner.

What needs to be challenged, of course, is the idea that the term 'family' presupposes heterosexuality. A gay or lesbian couple with or without adopted or artificially produced children, are as much of a family as a heterosexual couple. In countries that have legalized gay marriage, these couples can (and do) live exactly as heteronormative couples do. Many gay and lesbian couples all over the world have been accepted by their own extended families that include parents, grandparents, siblings, and near and distant relatives. In refusing to recognize such couples as a family, the UNHRC only perpetuates the stereotype of gays and lesbians as people incapable of serious, committed relationships, out to have sex with anonymous partners, contributing thereby to the spread of diseases like AIDS.

The gay marriage debate divides the gay community itself worldwide. The Vatican is opposed to the idea of gay marriage. It believes marriage to be a sacred rite that binds a man and a woman, but never two men or two women. The Vatican believes it to be the duty of all human beings to get married and produce children, unless of course they have vowed to be celibate. One pope once went on record to state that we needed to save the world from homosexuality, just as we needed to save our rain forests! The pro-gay marriage lobby within the gay community challenges the stand of the Vatican by refusing to subscribe to the idea that marriage exclusively involves people of opposite sexes. It takes marriage to be a union of hearts, minds and souls, and points out that the heart, mind, and soul have no gender. The pro-gay marriage lobby also regards the views of the Vatican as discriminatory, because it ensures that a gay couple cannot enjoy the same benefits as a heterosexual couple. For example, a married heterosexual couple can get a joint loan from a bank to buy a house or a car, and when one of them dies the other can receive his or her pension.

The anti-gay marriage lobby among gay people rejects the idea of gay marriage, but not for the same reasons as the Vatican. The definition of the terms 'husband' and 'wife' is socially constructed. Thus, the words husband and wife are socially and politically loaded. To be a husband traditionally means to be the breadwinner who goes out to work and to earn, and therefore to be in control of the property and the resources. To be a wife, conversely, implies being a homemaker, giving birth to children and raising them, not having an income and property of one's own, and not being paid for housework that is seen as a wifely duty. The watertight gender division that characterizes the words 'husband' and 'wife' breeds patriarchy. And patriarchy endorses the idea of male superiority and female inferiority. The unsatisfactory traditional definition of the words 'husband' and 'wife' is one reason why some gay people dismiss the idea of gay marriage. A gay couple does not want that one of them should be the husband who inhabits the outdoors and earns money, while the other is the wife who keeps house and looks after the family, and that too without being paid for one's services. At times, sexual behavior can perpetuate the stereotype even further, with one partner, usually the partner who goes out to work, being the penetrating or active partner, and the other partner being the penetrated or passive partner. To the anti-gay marriage lobby's way of thinking, patriarchy is imposed on a married gay couple by mainstream society, thereby frustrating their attempt to use their sexual orientation to dismantle stereotypes.

In *Love's Rite*, Ruth Vanita presents us with a scholarly account of same-sex marriage through the ages. What Vanita means by 'marriage' here is not the paperwork that we associate with it in courts and registries, but rather a symbolic union of hearts and minds. In such a scenario, the rituals and ceremonies that we associate with a wedding, such as circling the fire seven times and getting a priest to chant sacred verses, become relatively insignificant. For, a marriage is more than just these things. To Vanita, love is the key ingredient in marriage, more prevalent in same-sex marriage than in cross-sex marriage. She says, "All same-sex marriages are by definition love marriages, while most cross-sex marriages are family arranged" (Vanita, 2005: 29). To the extent that love is associated with eroticism, same-sex marriage is frowned upon because it foregrounds the erotic aspects of love. As discussed earlier, the opposition to same-sex marriage comes from both conservative and radical factions. However, Vanita's willingness to broaden the scope of the term 'marriage' insulates her against the attacks of radical queer theorists who oppose same-sex marriage on ideological grounds. According to them, "Marriage is a heterosexist, patriarchal institution not worth recovering because its history is fraught with the oppression of women and children" (Vanita, 2005: 22). These critics not only dislike the idea of same-sex marriage but also the idea of monogamy, which marriage presupposes. They argue that "monogamous coupling...is oppressive because it restricts sexual freedom and marginalizes single celibate and promiscuous people" (Vanita, 2005: 24). In other words, monogamy breeds monotony. Ruth

Vanita is married to Mona, to whom her book is dedicated, and the couple also has a son. Her book has photographs of other married same-sex couples of both genders. The female couples are Geeta Patel and Kath Weston who got married in America in 2004; Leela Namdeo and Urmila Srivastava, the famous policewoman couple of Madhya Pradesh who got married in the 80s; and Santosh and Manju of New Delhi. The lone male couple is Arvind Kumar and Ashok Jethanandani who got married in Canada in 1996.

As pointed out earlier, Vanita refers to *The Boyfriend* twice in her book. The first reference to it occurs when Vanita comments on the mock marriage of Yudi and Milind "who dress as bride and bridegroom for a private wedding ceremony" (Vanita, 2005: 179). In the second reference, Vanita discusses how the "gay protagonist, Yudi, a journalist, manages to retain his relationship with his working class boyfriend Milind only by supporting him financially, while Milind, who gets married to a woman, despises Yudi for his homosexual identity and single status" (Vanita, 2005: 244).

The mother of a New Bombay based gay activist, Harish Iyer, put a matrimonial advertisement on his behalf in a widely circulated tabloid newspaper. But the mother was not looking for a bride for her son. Instead, she was looking for a groom. This implied that her son was gay. In her advertisement, the mother went on to say that while the caste of the prospective applicant was no bar, an Iyer (Tamil Brahmin) would be preferred. This bit of conservatism on the part of an otherwise radical mother put her in a spot. However, to me, the mother's real orthodoxy was revealed in her desire to get her son married in the first place. In doing so, she was adopting a heteronormative institution as a template to negotiate her gay son's life. Harish Iyer's mother was not seeking to contest the idea of normativity itself. She was merely substituting heteronormativity with homonormativity, doing nothing thereby to dismantle the status quo. The mother was not using her son's sexual orientation as a peg to allow him to live his life creatively. As a hypothesis, if someone responded to the mother's ad, and the marriage was solemnized, would she regard the person as her son's husband or her son's wife? This was exactly the mother's dilemma in Karan Johar's *Dostana*. Would the couple be versatile in bed, or would one of them be active and the other passive? Would one of them be the breadwinner and the other the homemaker, or would both of them be breadwinners, or both homemakers? If the mother wanted to have a grandchild, as most Indian mothers do, would she ask her son and his husband/wife to adopt a child or to have a test-tube baby? Or would she advertise for a lesbian in the newspapers who could be a surrogate mother to her grandchild? If the marriage did not work out, how would the mother get it annulled? Going to court to ask for a divorce was out of question because, not just gay marriage, but homosexuality itself was illegal in India.

It is for these reasons that Gayatri Spivak once said in a 2007 talk at the Department of English, University of Pune, that gay marriage was "a writing back to heteronormativity."

Not many homosexual men and their families would, like Harish Iyer's mother, put matrimonial advertisements in the newspapers for same-sex spouses. What they would do, of course, is to get married to women without disclosing to the latter that they are gay. Homosexual men and women in India get married to people of the opposite sex in order not to be outed, and not to be ostracized. But this can prove costly, as case histories in India have recently shown. In one case, a woman who was married to a homosexual man installed spy cameras in their apartment in Bangalore and caught him having sex with men. She invoked Section 377 and got her husband imprisoned for life. It is true that the wife was wronged. Her husband betrayed her by marrying her in the first place, and then refusing to consummate the marriage. Instead, he made out with other men and exposed himself to the charge of adultery. Rather than getting married, the man should have resisted pressures brought upon him by his family to settle down. He should not have allowed the patriarchy to co-opt him, by learning to keep house and look after himself. The majority of Indian men, homosexual or otherwise, get married for domestic reasons. The wife in question suspected that her husband was gay when she found him using lip gloss. It is then that she began to observe him closely and was struck by his feminine mannerisms. However, it is difficult to believe that if the husband was effeminate, the wife did not notice this before getting married to him. Before she installed cameras in the house, the wife spoke to her neighbors. They informed her that in her absence (she worked in another town) her husband brought men home. The wife could have dealt with this by having a heart-to-heart talk with her husband and getting him to speak the truth. She could have asked him for a divorce, and perhaps even alimony. This approach would have at least saved the man from a prison sentence. To me, the approach that the wife chose is malicious. It is also homophobic and voyeuristic. It is well known that heterosexual men habitually titillate themselves with lesbian porn (see Chapter VI). Here the wife was doing this in reverse. She was a straight woman who was titillating herself with homosexual acts performed by her husband.

The ethics of installing cameras in the house are highly questionable. The Bangalore case is a throwback to an Aligarh Muslim University (AMU) case of 2010, where the university authorities installed hidden cameras in the apartment of a gay professor, Dr Shreenivas Ramachandra Siras. The footage showed the professor having sex with a 'lowly' rickshaw-wallah, leading to his suspension by the university. The shame of the episode, compounded by the unnecessary media attention that it received, caused the professor to commit suicide. However, a crucial difference between the AMU case and the Bangalore case is that the former happened in 2010, when the Delhi High Court judgment reading down Section 377 was still in force. Gay activists were thus able to approach the Allahabad High Court and get Dr Siras' suspension order quashed. The Bangalore case, on the other hand, happened in 2014, by which time the Supreme Court had overturned the Delhi High Court ruling.

The Allahabad High Court judgment in his favour not-withstanding, Dr Siras chose to commit suicide. A Bombay based movie director, Hansal Mehta, made a film titled *Aligarh* on Dr Siras's tragic story. Another film, Amol Palekar's *Quest* (*Thang* in Marathi, referred to in Chapter I) bore an uncanny resemblance to the Bangalore case. In *Quest*, Sai, Adi's US-educated lawyer wife, made life hell for him when she caught him in bed with Uday, Adi's openly gay best friend (and Sai's friend too). To start with, Sai's point of view in the film was exactly the same as the Bangalore wife's point of view. She felt that she had been cheated on two counts—one, his having an adulterous affair, and two, not revealing to her that he was gay. Both Adi and Uday went on a guilt trip after Sai's discovery of their illicit relationship. Uday, like the real-life Dr Siras, even contemplated suicide. After all, mainstream society would side with Sai and not with Uday, although both of them were victims. If, in the Bangalore case, the villain of the piece was a spy cam, in *Quest* it was a duplicate key with which Sai opened the door and entered the flat, when her flight to New York was unexpectedly cancelled.

In an interview in the anthology *Out*, Chitra Palekar, Amol Palekar's former wife, says of their own daughter Shalmalee:

> That makes me remember the time when my daughter came out. Only close family and friends knew. I really was keen to know what happens outside that circle. So I used to generally bring up the subject and then see what happened. Once, when I opened the topic, some people started talking about another girl they knew. They said, 'You know, she became a lesbian because she used to sleep in the same bed as her grandmother'.

(Hajratwala, 2012: 430)

The Bangalore case happened in 2014. The following year, 2015, another similar case was reported from Delhi. In this case, the wife got her homosexual husband arrested, but not under Section 377. Instead, he was arrested under Section 498 B, under which many married men and their families have been held. Since the wife committed suicide, leaving a suicide note on her Facebook page, the husband was also held under Section 304. In her suicide note, the wife said that her husband's homosexuality mentally tortured her. If the men in the Bangalore and Delhi cases had refrained from heteronormative marriage, four lives could have been happily led. In the latter case, the wife actually advised gay men in her suicide note to stay away from marriage. She is reported to have said: "If someone in society is like him [her husband] please don't marry a girl to save yourself, you people by doing so [are] not only playing with someone's emotions [but] also with a girl and her family's life." It is ironic that where she could have asked for a divorce, the Delhi wife stayed in the marriage for five long years. However, though the couple were doctors, they came from Rajasthan, a relatively conservative state. Resisting marriage, or once married, asking for a divorce is not easy in Rajasthan, and indeed in several parts of India, where marriage, as we know, is not between individuals, but between families and between clans. To spare themselves the shame of having to deal with homosexuality or divorce, such families often resort to emotional blackmail to force their children into submission.

Between homosexual men and women, it is men, I think, who have the rawer deal. Whether a married woman gets her gay husband arrested (as in Bangalore), or takes her own life (as in Delhi), the sympathy of mainstream society, and that of feminists, is always with her. If the tables are turned, and if the husband happens to be straight and the wife gay, mainstream society (and the feminists) will, in most cases, still side with the wife. To the feminists' way of thinking, the wife's turning to other women here is a comment on the misogyny, male chauvinism, and patriarchy that is widely prevalent in Indian society, as Manju Kapur's novel *A Married Woman* (2004) shows.

IV

Homosociality

In 1999, Penguin India, which had set up operations in the country in the late eighties, surprised the publishing industry and readers in general by issuing two potentially inflammable titles. The first was *Facing the Mirror* with the subtitle 'Lesbian Writing from India' (see Chapter VI); the second, *Yaraana* with the subtitle 'Gay Writing from India'. The former volume was edited by Ashwini Sukthankar, whom the book described as a Bombay based writer and activist born in Bombay in 1974 and educated at Harvard where she studied Comparative Literature. The latter volume, which exemplified the idea of homosociality, was edited by Hoshang Merchant, poet, Zoroastrian, with a PhD on Anais Nin from Purdue University in 1981. On returning to India, Merchant first taught at the University of Pune where he was victimized by the authorities on account of his sexuality, and then at the University of Hyderabad till his retirement in 2012. Mercifully, the two books did not create a controversy when they were released. They were not burned or banned. It is not as if they were not noticed—there were reviews of the two books in every major Indian newspaper and news magazine, and most of the reviews were favorable. However, the fact that the books were written in English, which is read by few, may have spared them the ordeal that Deepa Mehta's film *Fire* (made in both English and Hindi) suffered just the previous year (1998) when it was released in cinemas all over India. It has been more than fifteen years since *Facing the Mirror* and *Yaraana* were published. In 2010, Penguin India reissued an expanded *Yaraana* with a new subtitle: Gay Writing from South Asia. (To the best of my knowledge, *Facing the Mirror* has not been reissued.) In my capacity as a professor and a writer, I have lived with the two books these past eighteen years, using them as invaluable course material for courses I have offered in my own university (again, the University of Pune) as well as universities in Germany and Canada. Additionally, in the case of *Yaraana*, my own work—three poems from *BomGay* (2006) and two stories from *One Day I Locked My Flat in Soul City* (2001)—appears in it.

Yaraana was a radically different book from the sort of books published by mainstream Indian publishers for the following reasons: one, no mainstream Indian publisher had previously dared to bring out a compilation of gay writing, with the taboo word 'gay' in the title itself; two, no English language publisher in India had ever used a non-English word for a title. *Yaraana*, a Hindi word meaning 'friendship' was the title of a 1979 blockbuster Bollywood film, starring superstar Amitabh Bachchan. It finds a parallel in another Hindi word, *Dostana*, actually used by Bollywood director Karan Johar as the title of his 2007 film, which was a gay spoof. Merchant chose the word *yaraana* for his title on purpose. To him, the word represented that grey area between friendship and love for which the English language has no equivalent. While friendship is supposed to be platonic and nonsexual, love is sexual and romantic. The words *yaar* and *yaraana* refer to both friendship and love. While a straight man may refer to his (male) friend as his *yaar*, a straight woman may also refer to her (male) lover as her *yaar*. The word, then, is both generic and gender-neutral. As pointed out in Chapter I, in his essay titled "Yaari" (Ratti, 1993: 167–174), Raj Ayyar speaks of *yaari* as that which encompasses both the emotional and the sexual. He says, "There is really no English equivalent for this concept [*yaar*], no word that approaches its breadth and depth. *Friend* is not enough. *Buddy* is superficial...." Furthermore, "In India a world of romantic images revolves around *yaari*. There are tales of *yaar*s dying for one another [as in the Bachchan starrer *Yaraana*, referred to earlier, as well as in many other Bollywood films]. Even a wife must many a time take a backseat to a man's *yaar*." According to Ayyar, whose surname is almost an anagram of the word *yaar*,

> Even within a heterosexual context *yaar* has, and always has had, many homoerotic overtones, embodying values such as loyalty and strong commitment. A *yaar* is someone to whom one can reveal his darkest, deepest secrets. Thus one never has more than one or two *yaars* at one time. It is likely that during their early years a lot of *yaars* have had some sort of sexual connection before settling down to a socially accepted heterosexual life. They most often continue to express their physical affection openly, however; many a Western gay man has been puzzled by this, not realizing that the affection, for the most part, carries no overtones of sexuality.

In his Introduction to *Yaraana*, Merchant says, "India's Hindu culture which is a shame culture rather than a guilt culture, treats homosexual practice with secrecy but not with malice" (Merchant, 1999: xii). This implies that both homosexual and homosocial alliances are transgressive alliances that 'shame' not just the individual but the entire family, and society at large. Another of Merchant's oft-quoted views in his Introduction has to do with the 'universalisms' propounded, not by religion, not by bio-medicine, not by law, but by the mass media. He writes,

> In India, the MTV culture has done the country's homoerotic culture a disservice. It has projected plastic women like Sophiya Haq and Alisha Chinai onto the adolescent male imagination.... Your baker, butcher, banker, bus conductor, neighbor could all be very ordinary and also very gay.... It has also put many young men out of the gay circuit, forcing them prematurely into the arms of women.
>
> (Merchant, 1999: xiii)

In *Yaraana*, all the twenty or so contributors write under their own names. In terms of identity, the contributors to *Yaraana* are unabashedly gay. They thus attempt to mainstream themselves by taking on heteronormativity and substituting it with homonormativity. Again, they may be said to replace homophobia with 'heterophobia' and misogyny. Merchant's introductory remarks, quoted here, may be described as both 'heterophobic' and misogynist, for he describes women (such as Sophiya Haq and Alisha Chinai) as "plastic women," and complains about young men being prematurely driven into the arms of women, thereby depriving them of the right to choose with whom to sleep. Such a strain would also be present in many of the other selections in *Yaraana*, including Mahesh Dattani's play "Night Queen" (Merchant, 1999: 57–71), where the women in the play, who include Raghu's old mother and his sister Gayatri, are given no agency.

In his book *Sex/Text*, Hoshang Merchant says, "Gender is genre...the third gender will produce a third (new) genre, not prose, not poetry, not fiction, not fact, not discourse, not effusion, but a mixture of all these" (Merchant, 2009: 28).

Yet, we find that in *Yaraana* all the heavyweight male writers in the volume stick to the normative genres of literature. The list is as follows:

> **Poets:** Firaq Gorakhpuri, Sultan Padamsee, Namdeo Dhasal, Hoshang Merchant, Rakesh Ratti, Vikram Seth, Adil Jussawalla, Dinyar Godrej, R. Raj Rao, and others.
> **Fiction Writers:** Bhupen Khakhar, Kamleshwar, Firdaus Kanga, R. Raj Rao, and others.
> **Nonfiction Writers:** Ashok Row Kavi, Hoshang Merchant, Manoj Nair, and others.
> **Playwright:** Mahesh Dattani.

Thus, in terms of idiom, the majority of pieces in *Yaraana* with their expressive elegance and formal control would confirm to T. S. Eliot's dictum that "Poetry is not a turning loose of emotion, but an escape from emotion" (Eliot, 1976: 58).

Cultural differences between East and West make for some comic scenarios. Take the observed case of Indian men holding hands on the streets. No one thinks of this as odd because the men, after all, belong to the same gender (male), and hold hands in a spirit of camaraderie. In the West, people do not see it this way. There, if men held hands on the street, they would be making a statement about their gayness. Thus, Westerners who come to India for the first time often think of it as gay-friendly. An American homosexual once said to me, "In my country, I can walk hand-in-hand with my boyfriend only in the village [Greenwich Village in New York City] or on Castro Street [San Francisco]. Here, in India, you can do it anywhere, anytime." The American was right in his observations. However, he was wrong in his assumptions. Men do not hold hands in India for sexual or romantic reasons. They hold hands because they are homosocial. Confusions happen on account of heterosexism, which does not regard sexual attraction as gender-neutral. A man can only be sexually attracted to a woman, and a woman can only be sexually attracted to a man. In India, heterosexism often leads to the segregation of the sexes till marriage (and even after it), resulting in same-sex bonding among people. Homosocial segregation sometimes helps men and women to discover their homosexuality. It then becomes their alibi. Heterosexism must be contested, for it is based on easy generalizations and it straitjackets people. However, getting rid of it altogether also has its pitfalls. It can lead to a situation where *all* touch is perceived as sexual, as often happens in the West.

The jail is a vibrant homosocial space for same-sex sexual activity. Prison cells are always single-sex or monosexual enclosures where prisoners cannot make contact with people of the opposite sex. However, within these enclosures prisoners are often huddled together. Married inmates must necessarily lead celibate lives while their jail sentences are on. They discover an easy means of sexual gratification by turning to each other. Yet jail authorities are reluctant to acknowledge the existence of homosexuality in jails. One of the most famous of such denials in Indian prison history came from Kiran Bedi when she was superintendent of Delhi's Tihar Jail in the 1990s. Bedi refused to distribute condoms among the prisoners as, according to her, that would be tantamount to saying that homosexual activity existed in the jail. And Bedi was unwilling to acknowledge this as homosexuality is illegal in India. Thus, giving condoms to prisoners would bring Bedi into conflict with the law, though it would protect them from AIDS.

Student hostels in India are also monosexual spaces, like jails. In America, dorms, as they are called there, are no longer places where the genders are forcibly kept segregated. That is to say, a male student may choose to live with either a male or female roommate, and vice versa. If this still does not happen in American jails, it is because a jail sentence is meant to be punitive, and part of the punishment is to deprive prisoners of the solaces of sex. Homosexual sexual activity in monosexual places such as dorms and jails is sometimes referred to as 'situational homosexuality', a term I have used earlier. As I have previously pointed out, situations often serve as a catalyst to help people discover their true sexuality. Elsewhere, I have identified several other monosexual Indian spaces conducive to homosocial and homosexual activity. These, to recapitulate, are the *nukkad* or street corner, the male public urinal, the beer and country liquor bar, the *paan-beedi* shop, the gents' hair-cutting saloon, the taxi and auto-rickshaw stand, and the second-class local train compartment in cities like Bombay (Rao and Sarma, 2009: xx).

In the world Indian cinema, superstar Amitabh Bachchan remains the uncrowned prince of homosociality. I say this because in the 1970s he changed the grammar of Hindi cinema from romantic to homosocial. Much has been written by me and others about Bachchan's homosocial films of the 1970s. One film, *Sholay*, has merited so much discussion about its queer subtext, that whole dissertations have been attempted on it in Indian and foreign universities. In fact, I have myself given PowerPoint presentations on just one song from the film, which sees the two *yaars*, Jai and Veeru (Amitabh Bachchan and Dharmendra) ride together on a motorbike, even as iconic playback singers Kishore Kumar and Mohammad Rafi sing the song *Yeh dosti hum nahi todenge* picturized on them, to which they lip-sync. One of the questions that I ask in my PowerPoint presentation is, for example, whether the line *khana peena saath hai, marna jeena saath hai* in the song implies marriage, because it sounds exactly like a marriage vow. There are other lines and other visuals in the song that I similarly deconstruct.

In 2015, Sholay, which was released in Bombay's (now demolished) Minerva cinema on August 15, 1975, completed 40 years. Television channels invited Bollywood personalities to speak about the legendary film, and they included Dharmendra and Amitabh Bachchan themselves as well as Salim Khan and Javed Akhtar who wrote the film (as the famous Salim–Javed duo), and the director of the film, Ramesh Sippy. Even younger actors like Akshay Kumar reminisced about the film. Unfailingly, however, all the discussions revolved around the usual aspects of the film. Even though many of the discussions were moderated by film critic Rajeev Masand, there was no desire either on his part or on the part of the speakers to push the envelope and comment on the film's homosociality. Bollywood's reluctance to talk about the homosocial (or even homosexual) aspects of *Sholay* may be attributed to its homophobia (see Chapter V). Unlike in the gay Hollywood film *Brokeback Mountain*, in *Sholay* we rarely see Jai and Veeru by night. Most of the action takes place in broad daylight, considering that it is an outdoors film shot on location. Yet, the visuals and lyrics of the song quoted earlier, and indeed the film itself, is intriguing.

I have called Amitabh Bachchan the uncrowned prince of homosociality. Almost 40 years after *Sholay* and his other homosocial films of the 70s, we saw an ageing Bachchan in a homosocial role again, in the film *Shamitabh*. The title, which is a fusion of the first names of the two male actors in the film, Dhanush and Amitabh, speaks for itself. In *Shamitabh*, Bachchan gives the voice-impaired Dhanush his voice. But this is only a pretext for the two men to get together, hobnob with each other in the most solitary of settings such as a graveyard, a vanity van, and even a washroom where no one is around, and have 'lovers' squabbles. The washroom scene in the film is worth commenting upon. In queer theory, the washroom is a political space, a cruising site. Here, Bachchan sits on a potty in the washroom and sings for Dhanush who is lip-syncing just outside the washroom door. There is a heroine in *Shamitabh*, but she is a namesake heroine. As in *Anand*, *Sholay*, and *Namak Haraam*, some of Bachchan's homosocial films of the 1970s, in *Shamitabh*, the heroine, Akshara Haasan, seems to be there only because she *has* to be there. But the script conveniently dispenses with her every now and then by sending her off on jaunts, so that the two *yaars* can be left to their own devices. Of these 'devices' the most romantic one is left for the end. Bachchan and Dhanush are driving to a premiere, Dhanush at the wheel. And no, Akshara Haasan is not in the backseat. The banter, the singing (and even the flirting) that happens between the two men in the car is similar to such scenes in *Brokeback Mountain* and *Sholay*. The boyish Dhanush almost looks like the wizened Bachchan's catamite. The film, like *Anand*, *Sholay*, *Namak Haraam*, and *Brokeback Mountain* before it, ends tragically, with one of the two *yaars* losing his life.

Amitabh Bachchan looked awkward when he was cast in romantic films where he romanced his heroine in the rain and ran around trees with her. By the 70s and 80s, the audience for his films was predominantly male, young men in their twenties and thirties. Bachchan's films were perceived as 'action films' not quite suitable for women. In the 50s and 60s (the golden age of Hindi cinema), women in India frequented the movie theatres either with their men folk, or with other women. The love stories of the time were supposed to appeal to the emotional side of our natures, and women were regarded as emotional rather than rational beings. Their husbands and fathers thus gave them *permission*, as it were, to step out of the house and go to the cinema. With the onset of the action era, women's visits to the cinema decreased. They were convinced that films that abounded in fight sequences (*dishoom-dishoom* films, as they were called in India) were like stunt films, lacking in emotional content. The fights themselves were weaponless physical fights, necessitating much bodily contact between men. The changed perception also coincided with the advent of video. If women wanted to see *Sholay* and *Zanjeer* (and indeed Amitabh Bachchan was the heartthrob of many of them), all they had to do was borrow a video of the film from the neighbourhood video library and see it in the privacy of their own homes, far away from the lecherous catcalls of men in the cinema hall.

The homosocial bond that Amitabh Bachchan formed with other male actors on the screen was intensified by the presence of an all-male audience that had gathered to watch him. It engendered a sort of homoeroticism in the dark of the movie hall. Anyone who has been in a conventional cinema hall in India knows the conditions that prevail. In those days, the seats were narrow and cramped, worse than economy class seats in a Boeing 747, so that a maximum number of patrons could be accommodated. Air conditioning, more often than not, was nonexistent; even if the theatre was air conditioned, the air conditioners did not work on account of power cuts in the city. There were few electric fans in the auditorium (though there were plenty of human ones). As a result, body odours and the odour of betel spit permeated through the theatre and added to the sleazy atmosphere. If one took a look at the audience as the movie was showing (as I have frequently done), one was likely to find young men sprawled all over each other, clasping hands, putting arms around each other's shoulders and waists, even a leg on a leg, and more. Few of these men might have been consciously gay. Nor would they dare to exhibit such behavior if it were their women folk that were seated next to them. Same-sex closeness, as pointed out earlier, exists in every walk of Indian life, especially among the lower and lower middle classes. What conspires to give this a sexual coloration is, of course, that social mores do not permit men and women to be demonstrative with each other in public. Sex is strictly for procreation, not for recreation. Also, sex has little to do with love and romance. Every Indian thus grows up with a certain degree of sexual repression. Even if one is not *born* gay, it is very easy to *become* gay in India. However, to return to our audience of the 70s and 80s within the context of the movies they were viewing, their 'deviant' behavior in the cinema hall was sort of validated by the actions of their matinee idol. If Amitabh Bachchan could express undying love for other men on the screen, all in the name of *yaari*, why could not they too indulge in a little *masti*?

In the late 70s and early 80s, I was still in my twenties, studying—and later teaching—in colleges in Bombay. I had, by this time, discovered that I was gay. I often bought a ticket and went to an Amitabh Bachchan movie (yes, in those days he was my favourite actor too, and I even imitated him, our lankiness uniting us), not just to see him, but also in search of sexual adventure. Though the degree and intensity of my experiences varied, I rarely came back disappointed. At times, I went to the movie with a guy I had picked up at a park or a public loo, and throughout the movie we merely held hands. At other times, I found myself seated next to someone I fancied. As the lights went out, the action began, so to speak, both on the screen and off it. Frequently, my 'victims' readily yielded to my advances. For the next three hours or so, we had a good time, oblivious to the presence of people around us, who thought we were only *yaars*. Sometimes, if it was not a sold-out show, we discreetly moved to the middle or front of the theatre, where the empty seats offered us a measure of privacy. But it is not as if *I* was always the one who initiated the action. I distinctly remember the time when, half way through a movie, as I happened to glance at the guy sitting to my left, I found that he had flashed and was aroused, and was waiting expectantly for me to initiate sex. And not being the type who is accustomed to looking a gift horse in the mouth, I did. Later, the chap gave me lurid accounts of how men wanked each other in cinema halls, all while the film was on! Of course, I will be exaggerating if I suggest that I was always successful in these escapades in movie halls. I got my usual share of rebuffs and dirty looks from homophobic strangers (about whose homophobia I did not know), and a couple of times I was all but bashed up. However, I liked to look at the glass of water as half-full rather than half-empty.

I have spoken of homosocial segregation helping men discover their homosexuality. Such homosexuality, as we have seen, is dismissed by some queer theorists and activists as being merely 'situational'. Yet, I have spoken earlier of homosexual men using homosociality as their alibi. There is a silent pact at work here between homosociality and heterosexism. Heterosexism may be said to be the safety valve that prevents homosocial behavior from being read as homosexual. In India, two people of the same sex can be as 'physical' with each other as they please, and yet not be called homosexual. On the other hand, two people of the opposite sex *cannot* be 'physical' with each other, and not be called lovers. This is exactly what I demonstrate in my PowerPoint presentation of the *Sholay* song (referred to earlier). Amitabh Bachchan and Dharmendra are taken to be mere *yaars* because both of them belong to the same gender. However, if we retained the lyrics and visuals of the original song, and replaced Dharmendra with Hema Malini (who also acts in the film), would it still be possible to say that Amitabh Bachchan and Hema Malini are mere *yaars* (in the homosocial sense of the term)? Some heterosexual men detest the idea of homosociality being appropriated by gay men to camouflage their homosexuality. Such men want homosociality to retain its overtly nonsexual nature so that it is possible for two men to be buddies, without suspicion of their homosexuality being aroused in the minds of people. This, of course, is a Western reading of homosociality, caused by its divorce from heterosexism. Divorced from hetero-sexism, homosociality runs the risk of being interpreted as homosexuality, which some Western heterosexual men resent. In India, where heterosexism prevails in all walks of life, homosociality does not run the risk of being interpreted as homosexuality. The desirability of heterosexism, however, remains debatable. In queer theory, heterosexism is the objective correlative of what sexism is to feminists. If sexism smacks of gender bias, heterosexism hegemonizes the definition of 'natural', tyrannically seeing all gays and lesbians as 'unnatural'. Heterosexism thus encourages gays and lesbians to remain closeted, rather than to come out, because it is in closet alone that it would serve them as a safety valve. Raj Ayyar's notion of *yaari*, discussed earlier, is founded on the ambivalence that heterosexism combined with homosociality makes possible. It is a hallmark of Indian culture that defines our bonding patterns globally.

V

Homophobia

In *Love's Rite*, Ruth Vanita refers to what she calls India's "shame culture" (Vanita, 2005: 13). Likewise, Hoshang Merchant uses the term "shame culture" in his Introduction to *Yaraana* and posits it against the term "guilt culture" (Merchant, 1999: xii). While it is true that neither Vanita nor Merchant may have invented the term 'shame culture' and may have borrowed it from other sociologists, the term acquires relevance in the specific context of India's queer culture with its emphasis on family relations, its appropriation by Vanita and Merchant therefore being legitimate. The term 'shame culture' impacts homosexuality insofar as homosexuality, if made public, 'shames' not just the homosexual himself, but the entire extended family comprising parents, children, siblings, and relatives. Thus, homosexuality is frowned upon *only* if a person chooses to come out of the closet and lead a gay lifestyle, which implies, among other things, that he does not marry a woman. However, if he performs his 'duty' by getting married and starting a family, Hindu society seemingly has no qualms about his being a closeted homosexual. Merchant invokes the term 'shame culture' not just in relation to India, but to Hindu India, thereby imbuing it with religious significance. If shame is a legacy of Hinduism, itself sometimes described as a way of life rather than a religion, the concept of guilt flows directly from Christianity, with expiation and atonement being the only means of redemption. Thus, while the disrobing of Draupadi in the Mahabharata, or the abduction of Sita in the Ramayana, bring dishonor to their respective families, the crucifixion of Christ, for example, is a sinful act that must culminate in redemption if the sinner is not to be cast in hell. This brings us to the conclusion that while shame is familial, guilt is personal. Shame is rooted in the social and is tied up to cultures that are duty based, such as the culture of India. In the Bhagavad Gita, as is well known, Krishna implores Arjuna to go to war with his Kaurava cousins in the name of duty. Guilt, on the other hand, since it is rooted in the personal, is tied up to cultures that are rights based or individualist, such as the culture of the West. Two paradigms, then, roughly emerge:

Paradigm 1

> Shame—Family/Object—Society—Duty—Hinduism—India

Paradigm 2

> Guilt—Person/Subject—Individual—Rights—Christianity—West

Homophobia may loosely be defined as a prejudicial fear and hatred of homosexuality, homosexual people, and homosexual acts. This is not necessarily directed at others, but could also be directed at oneself. Many closeted homosexual men and women all over the world are found to be in denial about their sexuality on account of homophobia; in this case, both the homophobic subject and homophobic object are one and the same person. It is homophobia that causes such men and women to be in denial about their sexuality, and to remain in the closet. Homophobia may manifest itself in the form of physical and psychological persecution of the homosexual. Linguistically, expressions such as 'gay bashing' have come to be associated with homophobia. Here, the homosexual person is cornered and beaten up by a homophobic mob. The bashing may be so severe that it may result in death or permanent disability. In this case, the persecution is physical.

Psychological persecution may take the form of the family boycotting the homosexual person by refusing to speak to him. It may also include multiple forms of blackmail, as described further:

1. The homosexual person may be threatened to be outed to his family, neighbors, employers, and so on by the police, by hoodlums, or by a sexual partner met in a cruising area, or on the internet.
2. The family, especially the mother, may feign illness or threaten to commit suicide, etc., if the homosexual person does not marry and bring home a wife. And so on.

However, what I really wish to argue in this chapter is that homophobia does not exist in India. To establish this, I would like to start by making a distinction between the term 'homophobia' used in a purely cosmetic sense and the term 'homophobia' used in a technical sense. It seems to me that in India, we habitually use the word 'homophobia' in its cosmetic rather than in its technical sense. Thus, my previously mentioned descriptions of homophobia are only valid in the colloquial/cosmetic sense of the term, on which, I believe, we are heavily dependent on account of a lack of alternative terminology. And this can easily be managed with tactfulness and cunning when it pertains to society in general, and with bribery when it comes to hoodlums and the police. What abets this culturally is that in India one does not necessarily have to possess *one* sexuality to the exclusion of the *other*. In other words, one can fluidly be both heterosexual and homosexual at the same time. The precondition for homophobia is the straitjacketing of human beings as *either* homosexual or heterosexual. Hence, my contention is that the physical and psychological persecution of homosexuals, referred to earlier, does not really construe homophobia. My reasons for saying so are as follows:

1. The physical assaults of homosexual men have their equivalent among heterosexuals as well. Homosexuals cuddling up in a public place are not, as it were, bashed up *because* they are gay, but rather because they are perceived as indulging in 'indecent', 'immoral', and 'corrupting' acts. The culprits here, who could either be police constables, or hoodlums, or even ordinary members of the public, are driven by a misplaced sense of morality that stems from extreme orthodoxy and conservatism, and a lack of education. They are a part of what the media has come to refer to as the 'moral police'. But their ire is not restricted to homosexuals alone. As case studies in several of India's towns and cities have shown, heterosexual couples cuddling up in public places have been equally susceptible to violence on the part of the moral brigade. To term such violence as 'heterophobia' would be absurd. Yet, if the physical persecution of homosexuals is to be called homophobia, then, logically, the physical persecution of heterosexuals must be called heterophobia.

   A deeper analysis of the imperatives of the so-called moral police would reveal that it is not even an archaic sense of morality or decency, or a respect for the law of the land, which propels them towards acts of violence. What propels them, instead, is the opportunity for pecuniary gain and benefit that the trapping of victims affords. The victims themselves may come from socio-economic and socio-cultural backgrounds that foster a conservative mindset, so that at the end of the day, they are on the same page as their oppressors in the belief that they have erred. Hence, succumbing to the demands of their oppressors comes easy to them, and they offer little or no resistance. Once the oppressors' demands are met, let alone their (the oppressors') homophobia or heterophobia, even their alleged sense of morality vanishes into thin air, proving its dubious existence in the first place. The following autobiographical account should help me clinch my point. About twelve years ago, I was caught by policemen in the washroom of the Chhatrapati Shivaji (formerly Victoria Terminus) station in Bombay, well known as a cruising hotspot. The methodology employed by the policemen was to set an agent provocateur on me, himself a poor young homosexual captured by them a few minutes earlier, with no money on his person to pay for his release. The policemen thus decided to use him as a broker to solicit other victims. I was one such. Once I was caught, I knew that resistance was useless. The cops, after all, had the law on their side; this was a time prior to July 2009 when the Delhi High Court had read down Section 377 of the IPC to exclude consenting adults from its purview. So, I did what I thought logical in the circumstances: I opened my wallet and offered the policemen (as many as five in number) money. But the money I had in my wallet was insufficient for them. Noticing a set of credit and debit cards sticking out of my wallet, the cops, after slapping me repeatedly across my face, ordered me to accompany them to an ATM booth to withdraw cash that would satisfy all of them. In 2005, it was ₹5000; today, it would obviously be much more. In one respect, however, I was lucky: the policemen did not insist on checking the balance in my account, which, needless to say, would have tempted them to rip me off of much more than they actually did. But my story does not end here. I am really concerned in narrating what happened in the aftermath of money exchanging hands. To my utter surprise, the policemen fished out a long list of mobile phone numbers of homosexual men and asked me to store the numbers in my own phone. *The numbers will help you gratify your desires*, they almost said to me as they took my leave, the telltale slap marks still on my face.

The cops who got me at the Bombay train station, then, cannot be said to be homophobic. If they were, they would not have passed on the mobile phone numbers of other homosexual men to me. Before parting, they added *my* mobile number to their list. Their activities establish that they have hit upon a foolproof technique to supplement their meager incomes. The issue, thus, is one of corruption rather than of homophobia.

2. To move now from the physical to the psychological persecution of homosexuals, my contention is that, here too the term 'homophobia' to define what happens is inaccurate. Let me return to the idea of India as a shame culture. As stated earlier, within a joint family set up, it is not homosexual acts in isolation that are perceived as bringing dishonor to the family. Heterosexual acts are capable of doing the same, if the relationship is between couples of different castes, or class backgrounds, or religions, or even if a large age difference separates them (in India, a ten-year age difference is considered to be indecent). The sense of dishonor that a family suffers on account of 'transgressive' heterosexual alliances cannot, of course, be called 'heterophobia'. Actually, in the case of heterosexuals, the management of honor turns out to be more difficult than in the case of homosexuals, because heterosexuals have the institution of marriage. Thus, if the transgressing couple insists on getting married, it may attract the attention of what have come to be known

as the 'khap panchayats', who may ostracize the couple to the point of death by murder or by suicide. There are instances in Indian states such as Kerala and Haryana where, acting independently, or at the behest of the khap panchayats, parents are known to have tracked down their transgressing offspring and slaughtered them, like livestock. This is the theme of the popular Marathi film *Sairat* (2016, director Nagraj Manjule). As stated earlier, the business of honor among heterosexuals is hard to manage because of the prevalence of the institution of marriage. Arguably, it would have been easier if the couple in question chose to have 'honorable' marriages in deference to the wishes of their parents, and then continued to have a secret adulterous relationship with each other. This is where homosexuality has an edge. If human sexuality exists on a spectrum, or as the Kinsey Study explained it, on a six-point scale, it implies that the majority of human beings have elements of both heterosexuality and homosexuality in them. In other words, the majority of human beings are bisexual. In India, our way of acknowledging this is to not put the two binaries of hetero/homo into boxes, but to allow them to overlap. Thus, few homosexuals in India opt out of heterosexual marriage. The marriage itself is an 'arranged' marriage, with the homosexual subject readily giving his consent to marrying the girl chosen for him by his parents, and possibly his extended family. Once the marriage is solemnized, the homosexual subject is a normative subject to all intents and purposes. He is now free to live a closeted homosexual life in addition to a heteronormative life, to which no one is witness. Admittedly, the homosexual male has it easier here than the homosexual female, because patriarchy and misogyny—integral parts of the culture—validate and valorize his dual life. The khap panchayats are not after the homosexual subject simply because they know nothing (or are not supposed to know anything) about his closeted gay life, even as there is nothing subversive about the visible face of his heterosexual life.

Sushil Patil, one of the respondents in my book *Whistling in the Dark* is a typical such homosexual subject. He lives in small-town Maharashtra, teaches at a local college, and is married with two grown-up children. Sushil claims that though he has been married for nearly twenty years; his wife, a school teacher, does not know about his (closeted) homosexuality, and the issue has never come up between them. This is in spite of the fact that Sushil's personality, including his voice and style of walk, has clearly effeminate traits in it. When I last met Sushil, a few years after my book was published, he told me that he had packed off his wife and children to the city, the ostensible reason for this being the education of his children. He, on the other hand, held on to his job at his rural college and had gotten an undergraduate male student to move in with him. Sushil's relationship with the student was unabashedly sexual. Yet, as far as the college authorities were concerned, it came across to them as an act of charity and kindness on Sushil's part, because the student in question was poor and needy. To the college authorities, Sushil allowed the boy to lodge and board with him because he could not afford to stay at a hostel and eat in a mess! This alibi also convinced Sushil's wife and college-going kids, now living in the city a few hundred kilometers away from Sushil's town.

Why is Sushil able to establish an alibi? Heterosexism provides the answer. Heterosexism, as explained in Chapter IV, is the belief that sexual attraction is gender-specific and not gender-neutral. In other words, the precondition for sexual attraction is that the persons concerned must belong to opposite sexes and not to the same sex. If two persons of the same sex exhibit intimacy in public (such as walking hand in hand, or with arms around each other's shoulders and waists), that must be taken to be a sign of their *yaari* and *dosti* (Indian words for friendship), and in some cases, *masti* (mischief). If they live together, they must be taken to be roommates— nothing less, nothing more. On the other hand, if the persons concerned belong to opposite sexes, it is immediately taken to be sexual. Heterosexism, as pointed out earlier, is today a uniquely Eastern phenomenon. It exists all over the Eastern world. However, in the West, sexual attraction is no longer regarded as gender-specific. Hence, the extermination of homosexuals in the concentration camps in Nazi Germany, and the persecution of homosexuals in Greenwich Village, New York City, prior to the Stonewall riot of 1969. As stated in Chapter IV, this crucial cultural difference between East and West can sometimes lead to comic (and cosmic) confusion, as first time Westerners in India who see our men walking hand-in-hand on our streets, and that too in broad daylight, think of India as a gay haven or gay paradise. In their own cities, they would only be able to exhibit such behavior in designated spaces, such as, for example, the Village in New York City, Castro Street in San Francisco, or Church Street in Toronto. Thus, to return to Sushil Patil, he was able to live the kind of dual life he lived (and continues to live) on account of the protective shield of heterosexism. I would argue that heterosexism provides the perfect antidote to homophobia by attacking and destroying its very foundations. It guards the homosexual subject from being recognized and identified, and camouflages his public behavior.

Much has been written on the pluralism of sexual behavior in precolonial India by scholars such as Ruth Vanita, Saleem Kidwai, Giti Thadani, and Devdutt Pattanaik, with even popular writers like Chetan Bhagat chipping in. As evidence, they have cited stories with a queer subtext from our myths and mythologies, they have invoked ancient works like the *Kamasutra*, and have spoken of the temple sculptures at

Khajuraho and Konarak. Chetan Bhagat quotes a line from the *Rig Veda* that says, "Vikruti evam Prakriti," which he translates into English as "perversity/diversity is what nature is all about, or what seems unnatural is also natural." (Bhagat, *The Times of India*, September 6, 2014). Likewise, in "The Contract of Silence" in *Yaraana*, Ashok Row Kavi speaks of how when he came out to his guru, the latter told him that the soul has no gender (Merchant, 1999: 2–25). I would like to borrow the metaphor of amnesia or loss of memory, used by the critic G. N. Devy for the title of his award-winning book *After Amnesia* (1992) in the context of India's *bhasha* literatures, to define what destroyed the pluralism of Indian sexuality during the colonial period. Before Lord Macaulay introduced British India's infamous anti-gay law of 1869, he also made English education in India compulsory (vide his Minute on Education of 1835). The imperatives behind both moves were identical— they had to do with a cleansing of the 'decay' that had set in, whether linguistically or sexually, in the colony (Rao and Sarma, 2009: xxiii). (Incidentally, the anti-gay or antisodomy law, as pointed out earlier, was simultaneously introduced in all of England's colonies at more or less the same time, and was called Section 377 everywhere.) Macaulay's act of cleansing also amounted to an act of erasure. The British succeeded in wiping our memories clean of all traces of the past to such an extent that today, ironically enough, it is the Hindu revivalist groups and Hindu revivalist political parties that argue that homosexuality is against Indian culture, whereas they should actually be concerned with reviving ancient and medieval India's pluralist sexual culture. However, their public pronouncements are at odds with the collective consciousness of the people that seems to hark back instead to precolonial times. Homophobia simply cannot exist in a culture that still endorses the system of arranged marriages, which involves the segregation of boys and girls till their families find a suitable match for them. There is a contradiction in the claim that homosexuality is against

Indian culture and the physical closeness of men in public places that is not regarded as a taboo. To me, there can be no stronger proof of the fact that homophobia is not integral to the culture of India.

Many statements made by Ruth Vanita prove (but also refute) my contention. Quoting a Tata Institute of Social Sciences study of 2003, conducted by Bina Fernandez and N. B. Gomathy, Vanita writes:

> The extreme homophobia we witness today, manifested in beatings and murders of gay people in the West, public executions in the Middle East, violence against gay people and calls to persecute them in many countries, including India and Nepal, is a product not of the ancient or medieval past, but rather of modernity.
>
> (Vanita, 2005: 13)

Vanita points out that although homosexuality was condemned in medieval Europe, it was regarded as a sin rather than as a crime. It was only after the Renaissance, from the 14th century onwards, that homosexuality came to be regarded as a crime, and became the business of the State rather than of the church. Likewise, speaking of America, Vanita says, "Native Americans were much more tolerant of same-sex relationships, but their cultures were steamrollered by that of the colonizers" (Vanita, 2005: 14). In India, according to Vanita, "Under colonial rule, what was a minor strain of homophobia in Indian traditions became the dominant ideology [under British rule]" (Vanita, 2005: Ibid). To Vanita, in India:

> ...modern homophobia is deeply intertwined with modern nationalism. Most Indian nationalists, who fought for Indian independence from British rule, including M. K. Gandhi, [uncritically] accepted the rulers' view of homosexuality as a vice. Indian nationalists today, both right wing and left wing, are often virulently homophobic, viewing homosexuality as a foreign disease or capitalist perversion from which the nation's purity must be preserved. Several Indian politicians and opinion makers defend Section 377 as 'Indian' and call for even

stronger measures against homosexuality, which they declare as a product of the West.

(Vanita, 2005: 15–16)

Vanita's final point is that:

...modern homophobia, in India as in England, is most evident in the middle classes who shape educated public opinion, and less evident among the former aristocracy and the poor. Homophobia drives many Indians to lead double lives, flee the country, try to 'cure' themselves, or even commit suicide.

(Vanita, 2005: 16)

In the Christian West, homosexuality traditionally has been viewed as a sin. This breeds a kind of religious homophobia that cannot be dealt with by simple worldly tools. The Vatican's homophobia goes to such an extent that, as pointed out earlier, it once stated that the world had to be saved from homosexuality, just as its rain forests needed to be saved: failure to save the world from either the one or the other would lead to its destruction. A sin must be atoned for, or expiated, without which the sinner remains guilty for life, and upon death goes to hell. This is how the culture of the West becomes a 'guilt culture'. The orthodox are shocked by the fact that the world has become so 'degenerate' today that it argues for same-sex marriage and upholds homosexuality even in its most perverse forms (see Chapter VII).

In America, the famous Matthew Shepard case of 1998 helps us understand the difference between real and imagined homophobia. On the night of October 6, 1998, 22-year-old Matthew Shepard was offered a ride by Aaron McKinney, also 22, and Russell Henderson, 21, whom he had met at the Fireside Lounge, a gay bar in Laramie, Wyoming. (Incidentally, Wyoming State is the setting of the gay film *Brokeback Mountain*.) McKinney and Henderson drove Matthew into the wilderness in their truck, where they beat him up so brutally that his skull was fractured and his face was covered in blood. They then tied him up to a fence and drove off. When Shepard was discovered 18 hours later by Aaron Kreifels, a cyclist who thought he was a scarecrow; he was in a coma. Eventually Shepard succumbed to his injuries a week later. On the face of it, the motive for the murder was robbery. McKinney and Henderson, though not gay themselves, pretended to be gay and went to the Fireside Lounge in search of victims. When police officer Flint Waters arrested McKinney, he found Shepard's shoes and credit card in his truck. Yet, we must keep in mind that Shepard was only a youngster, and could not have had much money either on his person or in the bank at the time of the attack. Why then did McKinney and Henderson choose him, when there would have been richer patrons at the Fireside Lounge? That homophobia, and not robbery, was the principal reason for Matthew Shepard's murder is borne out by two facts. One, McKinney's girlfriend Kristen Price's statement to the police that McKinney was motivated by anti-gay sentiment, by how he "felt" about gays. (However, Price was later made to withdraw this statement and say that she had lied because she thought it would save McKinney.) Two, McKinney's own press interview in which he claimed that Henderson and he had only intended to rob Shepard, and not kill him, and that the killing was triggered by Shepard's homosexual act of putting his hand on McKinney's knee in the truck. Though this view was rejected by the court, and by the media, a police officer, Dave O'Malley, who was in charge of the case, said, "I feel comfortable in my own heart that they did what they did to Matt [Matthew] because they had hatred toward him for being gay" (Source: Wikipedia).

VI

Lesbianism

Although *Facing the Mirror* and *Yaraana* are both anthologies of writing based on the theme of same-sex love, the resemblance between the two books ends there. The two anthologies, when read in conjunction with each other, enable us to see that the terms 'lesbian/gay' and 'queer' which most lay people believe to be synonymous with one another are actually radically different formulations in terms of the theories they represent. The two books, then, when properly conceptualized should make it possible for us to ask of non-heterosexual people whether they are lesbian/gay OR queer, just as we might ask people if they are straight/heterosexual or gay/homosexual. Let us turn to two constructs used by Sukthankar in her Introduction to *Facing the Mirror*. These are the constructs of 'lesbian' (which, for the purposes of my argument, would also include the construct 'gay') and that of 'writing'. The first construct is concerned with the question of identity, the second with that of language. Sukthankar uses a third construct, namely 'Indian', which concerns the question of nationality. I shall not touch upon this here, though it also has serious ramifications for the politics of sexuality in India, especially because, as Ruth Vanita says, in India "modern homophobia is deeply intertwined with modern nationalism" (Bose and Bhattacharya, 2007: 347).

Sukthankar says about her project, "When we talk of 'Indian lesbian writing' the term is in conflict with itself; the very theme which tries to draw this book into a whole is challenged from within by the words and lives of the women who wrote for it" (Sukthankar, 1999: xviii).

A fundamental difference between *Yaraana* and *Facing the Mirror* is that while, as pointed out in Chapter IV, all the twenty or so contributors to the former write under their own names, and reveal their surnames or last names, the majority of contributors to the latter write under assumed names or pseudonyms, and in any case use only first names. The only (well-known) contributors who use their real names, together with their last names, are Ashwini Sukthankar, Giti Thadani, Ruth Vanita, Mita Radhakrishnan, and a few others. This implies, for one, that the majority of contributors to *Facing the Mirror* are not out of the closet, for there is a close connection between naming and identity, and for lesbians to conceal their true names may indicate that for them their sexual preference for persons of their own gender does *not* constitute an identity. As one contributor to the anthology, quoted earlier, puts it, "I just want to *be* gay; I don't want to attend conferences about it" (Sukhthankar, 1999: xxix). Or, to formulate that differently, lesbians and gays who derive their identity from their sexuality must of necessity come out of the closet. Furthermore, an assumed name or pseudonym is also, at the end of the day, an alias. Aliases are frequently used by persons whom the State would define as 'criminals' or 'terrorists'. Thus, the lesbian contributors to *Facing the Mirror*, unlike the gay contributors to *Yaraana*, are willing to see themselves as outlaws.

This is where the antithetical words 'lesbian/gay' and 'queer' come into play. In marked contrast to the minoritizing words 'lesbian/gay', the universalizing term 'queer' refers to a destabilizing of (hetero)normativity, achieved through an all-encompassing resistance to norms. The basic characteristic of queerness is that it is opposed to replacing one form of normativity with another. The moment anything that begins as a resistance to norms becomes a norm in itself, it ceases to be queer, and it is up to the queer subject to negotiate the tricky business of normativity in such a way that the decentralizing trait of queerness is not lost. By using assumed names/pseudonyms/aliases, the contributors to *Facing the Mirror* may be said to endorse the oppositional idea of Gay Shame. In doing so, they succeed in destabilizing both normativity and heteronormativity, emerging as women with a queer 'identity' rather than a lesbian identity.

The other construct used by Sukthankar is that of 'writing'. As pointed out in Chapter IV, Hoshang Merchant says, "Gender is genre...the third gender will produce a third (new) genre, not prose, not poetry, not fiction, not fact, not discourse, not effusion, but a mixture of all these" (Merchant, 2009: 28). The statement, I believe, could not apply more to the selections in *Facing the Mirror.* Let us begin by posing a question: What is writing? The literary establishment would probably answer the question by informing us that writing is (published) poetry, fiction, drama, and nonfiction, to cite its most prominent forms. Now let us examine what editor Sukthankar has to say about the selections included in *Facing the Mirror.* She writes,

> The pieces that were produced for this book...might not be writing in the purist's sense.... Women sent in poems scribbled on scraps of paper and hidden away for years, extracts from journals, love letters—astonishing artifacts in a world which consumes and discards the written word like any other mass-produced commodity. Other women asked if they could record their narratives on tape for us to transcribe, since they were either not literate, or had spent so many years using the written word as a shield of prevarication, that writing to reveal and express had become impossible. Again, it might be argued that this genre, whatever it is, is not writing. But for the purposes of this compilation, 'writing' signifies the gritty imperfect media through which the body, with its yearning and its suffering, spoke out; the process through which our lives, put into the tangibility of words, could be made public.
>
> (Sukthankar, 1999: xxi)

In a way it is ironic that Ashwini Sukthankar with her degree in comparative literature from Harvard University should be the editor of *Facing the Mirror.* This is because presumably at Harvard, what would be admissible into the curriculum would be the canonical text rather than the queer text, with strict emphasis on the normative genres of writing—poetry, fiction, drama, and nonfiction. This is not to suggest that, Sukthankar's disclaimers notwithstanding, none of the pieces in *Facing the Mirror* qualify as 'writing' in the conventional sense. Yet, a close reading of the poem "Leaving" (Sukthankar, 1999: 73), for example, by a poet who simply uses the initials A. G. in place of her name, gives one the feeling that the poem is no poem because it has neither rhyme, nor meter, nor imagery, nor figures of speech, but reads rather like chopped prose:

> *We strain against each other,*
>
> *She, trying to thrust me out*
> *Me, stubbornly resisting.*
> *I want to stay with you...please*
>
> *I don't know the world outside*
> *I can't face it on my own*
> *I'm not yet ready*
> *ready to be born.*
>
> *Mm, mm...Dhuk, dhuk*
> *Muffled sounds filter through*
> *to relieve the monotony*
> *of her frantic screams and keening.*
>
> *She is wiser*
> *and bigger and stronger than me—*
> *it's a losing battle—*
>
> *I'm out!*
>
> *No wonder I feel like crying.*

The language construct of *Facing the Mirror* goes beyond the issue of genre. It also concerns the idiom employed by the writers, which is not 'decorous' but 'gross', as the following evocative passage from "The Complete Works of Someshwar P. Balendu," referred to in Chapter II, shows:

> As soon as I was old enough to find out where it could be done, I had my breasts cut off...I begged the nurse to give me something for the pain. More, I begged, more, more. The syringe pricked me once, twice, thrice, the blessed prongs of the trishul of the lord of yogis, om om om. Then I was able to close my eyes and let the agony flow into a mirror of glass...
>
> I forgot how long they kept me there, in the filthy general ward. The bandage became stiff as a Kurukshetra warrior's shield. Thread by thread I pulled it loose from my wound. All around me the suffering people called upon deaf gods for water, for mercy, for death...
>
> I was not sure, but I thought my breasts might have been thrown into the municipal dustbin, buried in mango peels, egg shells, tea leaves and crusted sanitary napkins until dogs or a sweeper's broom found them, ripening in the heat...
>
> My cousin...told me about a villager who worked on her uncle's farm. One hand was pulled into a threshing machine during harvest. Chopped off completely. Someone picked it up from the wet red wheat but stole the ring. The villager screamed all the way to the district hospital, carrying the hand in her father's turban.
>
> (Sukthankar, 1999: 271–272)

This distinction between 'subtle' and 'gross' writing applies to other forms of 'marginal' literature as well, such as Dalit literature, especially in Marathi. (The late playwright Vijay Tendulkar once confessed at a book launch in Bombay, for example, that he rebuffed the Dalit poet Namdeo Dhasal who approached him with his poem "Golpitha," saying that he did not understand his idiom, which was 'crass'. This, though both writers wrote in the same language—Marathi). The conclusion that we must come to, then, is that if gender equals genre, then it is the women writers in *Facing the Mirror* rather than the male writers in *Yaraana* who successfully produce a queer text.

Judith Butler, as we know, speaks of gender as performance, based on an authoritative naturalization of heterosexuality. She rejects the idea of a queer continuum because feminism, whose agenda is gender equality as opposed to sexuality per se, subsumes lesbianism, thereby perpetuating the male/ female binary among gays/lesbians (Butler, 1994: 1–26). Taking her cue from Butler, Ranjita Biswas points out that mainstream feminists are "reluctant to re-examine the notion of naturalized heterosexuality" (Bose and Bhattacharya, 2007: 278). By deduction, then, the patriarchy prevalent in mainstream heterosexual society is replicated in LGBT (lesbian-gay-bisexual-transgender) society. Perhaps that is why the identities of the gay writers in *Yaraana* and the lesbian writers in *Facing the Mirror* are so radically different—the former moving towards an essentialist homonormativity and the latter concerned with an anti-essentialist destabilizing of heteronormativity. That is why, although the two anthologies came out at the same time, around the turn of the century, and were published by the same publishing house, they are poles apart in structure, execution, and design.

To Foucault, it will be recalled, to be set on being gay would mean that one uses one's gayness as a peg with which to perceive things creatively, and lead a creative lifestyle that would translate into and cover the entire gamut of activities from artistic designer living to sexual experimentation. It is here that gays and lesbians often come into conflict with one another and render the likelihood of a queer continuum impossible. This is because, as Ranjita Biswas explains, the supposed affinity of gay men (referred to in Chapter III) "for sexual pleasure as evident from their investment in anonymous lovers, pederasty and their preoccupation with ageist standards of sexual attractiveness has drawn flak from lesbian activists and feminists alike" (Bose and Bhattacharyya, 2007: 278). While mainstream feminists would interpret this as patriarchy, no different from the patriarchy (and double standards) of straight men, lesbians would tend to view it as promiscuity, responsible, among other things, for the AIDS pandemic in India and other parts of the world. Promiscuity becomes synonymous with patriarchy by this formulation, and unites both lesbians and feminists in their condemnation of male homosexuals as men with scant respect for stable, committed relationships. And what makes gay men more gullible than their straight counterparts is the fact that the potential for 'sleeping around' among the latter is at least held in check by the institution of marriage, with its conventions of fidelity and monogamy. Gay men have no such bindings.

In the popular TV serial *Emotional Atyachaar*, aired on UTV Channel, the majority of episodes featured men as cheaters who cheated on their girlfriends/wives, while only a fraction of the episodes portrayed women as cheaters. Thus, in imitating mainstream heterosexual women in their need for emotional stability, and their social censure of most forms of transgressive sex, the lesbians, including those who have contributed to *Facing the Mirror*, face a contradiction. What they need to negotiate is if normativity, including heteronormativity, can be destabilized by its very antithesis—stability.

In Axiom 2 of *Epistemology of the Closet* (see Chapter II), Eve Sedgwick speaks of the study of sexuality as not being coextensive with the study of gender and of anti-homophobic inquiry not being coextensive with feminist inquiry. However, the concept of 'political lesbianism', a term used by Barbara Ryan (2001) may be an attempt to straddle the categories of sexuality and gender. Political lesbians are different from women whose natural sexual preference is for people of their own sex. Yet, they are also different from heterosexual women and mainstream feminists, whose gender rights may be said to be neutralized (or compromised) by their sexual dependence on men. Political lesbianism is defined by its social bonding patterns, rather than by sexual preference; the emphasis is on homosociality (see Chapter IV), rather than on homosexuality. In India, the terms *saheli* and *sakhi* may be used to understand the phenomenon of political lesbianism; these words may be said to be the equivalent of the homosocial term *yaar*, discussed in Chapter IV. A typical political lesbian would be one who turns to the opposite sex for sexual gratification, while she turns to her own sex for social, emotional, and even romantic sustenance. Political lesbianism exists on a "lesbian continuum," a term of course made famous by Adrienne Rich (Sedgwick, 1990: 36), along with lesbianism per se and mainstream feminism.

Axiom 3 of *Epistemology of the Closet* reads as follows:

> There can't be an a priori decision about how far it will make sense to conceptualize lesbian and gay male identities together. Or separately.
> (Sedgwick, 1990: 36–39)

The term 'lesbian continuum' used previously, implies, for one, that lesbians have more in common with women than with gay men. For, as Sedgwick explains, lesbian sexual object choice embodied a "specificity of female experience and resistance." Lesbian sexual object choice is obviously not symmetrical with gay male sexual object choice. That is to say, while lesbians desire women, gay males desire men. Feminist intervention also posited male and female experiences and interests as *different* and *opposed*, swinging the lesbian vote in favor of feminism. Thus, in Sedgwick's view, "an understanding of male homo/heterosexual definition could offer little or no...interest for any lesbian theoretical project" (Sedgwick, 1990: 37). By this formulation, an antihomophobic reading of lesbian desire automatically led to a homophobic reading of gay male desire. However, this was reformulated in the late 1970s with the realization "that lesbians and gay men shared important though contested aspects of one another's histories, cultures, identities, politics and destinies" (Sedgwick, 1990: 37). Lesbians disagreed with the high moral ground adopted by mainstream feminists with regard to sexual deviance in general, and pornography and S/M in particular. Transgender (gay) men and (lesbian) women discovered that their identities had been constructed through, and in relation to, one another. At this juncture, AIDS made its appearance and irretrievably polarized heterosexuals and homosexuals of all genders. AIDS fostered a negative reading of the category of the 'pervert' (see Chapter VII). Since the AIDS virus was believed to spread through unprotected anal sex between gay men, lesbians, according to

Sedgwick, should have felt a "relative exemptive privilege." Yet they did not. Sedgwick here calls mainstream society that refused to distinguish between lesbians and gays their "enemies." Though lesbians were not directly affected by AIDS, the hostility of mainstream society, including feminists, caused them to join gay men in LGBT activism. Ironically, it was feminist perspectives on medicine and health care, as Sedgwick informs us, which came in handy here in the lesbians' efforts to contain AIDS. Even so, Sedgwick leaves the question of a gay–lesbian continuum open-ended. She feels that this can only be achieved in "an alternative, feminocentric theoretical space…" (Sedgwick, 1990: 39). Still, she cautions us that "the extent, construction, and meaning, and especially the history of any such theoretical continuity—not to mention its consequences for practical politics—must be open to every interrogation."

In the early 2000s, five Poona-based women got together to form a lesbian support group called OLAVA. The name was actually an acronym that stood for Organized Lesbian Alliance for Visibility and Action. It was a brave move, given the prejudice that lesbians face. The group was said to have had its first meeting in the home of one of the women, with the blessings of her parents. It was one of the first lesbian collectives of its kind. The OLAVA women wanted to form a coalition of gay support groups all over India to fight for their rights. But this did not kick off. Most gay support groups in India (with the exception of support groups like Kolkata's Sappho for Equality) were male gay support groups, towards whom the members of OLAVA were hostile. Women who love women are denounced by men and women, gay and straight alike. Straight men commodify lesbians, fantasizing about what they do in bed. They often find lesbian porn more titillating than heterosexual porn. Once, when traveling in rural Maharashtra, I put a copy of *Facing the Mirror* in my backpack to review. I showed the book to a straight male friend with whom I was staying, who taught at a mofussil college. Later in the day, the friend, without my knowledge, photocopied passages from the book that excited him. One of them was an explicit description of how two women licked each other's pussies. Likewise, straight women feel that lesbianism is not an important-enough issue in the fight for women's empowerment and gender equality, and also that it is against Indian culture. Gay men resent the fact that Section 377 of the IPC applies only to them and not to lesbians, considering that it is concerned with penetrative sex. Thus, as Ranjita Biswas says, "...a recurring theme in lesbian theoretical writings has been the relational chasm that separates lesbians and/or lesbianism from other identities, groups and movements like heterosexual feminism, gay liberation and queer politics" (Bose and Bhattacharyya, 2007: 278). That leaves the lesbians with no one to turn to for succor, except themselves. This is proved by two recent case studies. The first case study concerns two women in Etapalli village in Maharashtra's Gadchiroli district, known for its Naxalite presence. They were neighbors and they fell in love. Let us call the two women Shabana and Nandita, the former in her thirties and the latter in her twenties. Shabana was married off by her parents and had children. But Shabana's husband was an alcoholic. Nandita, still unmarried, moved in with Shabana. They raised Shabana's two children, a son and a daughter, together. The people of the village began gossiping. To save their 'honor', Nandita's parents got her married. She had a son. Now Nandita wanted her husband to let Shabana stay with them, to which he did not agree. As for Shabana, her husband stopped having sex with her. The bedroom in their house was reserved for Shabana and Nandita. The two women wanted to move out of the ambit of heteronormativity and set up a home together. They attempted to elope, not once but twice. But their families stepped in and compelled them to go back to their respective husbands. Shabana's husband ordered her to sever all relations with Nandita. Instead, she asked him for a divorce. Shabana and Nandita began living together in Etapalli. Although conservative society did not allow them to rent a house and start a business in Etapalli, they defied society and continued to live together as a couple.

The second case study took place in Uttar Pradesh. A district court sentenced a lesbian couple, Kamala Devi and Shanta Devi, to life imprisonment. They were arrested not because they were lesbians, but because they were accused of murdering Kamala Devi's husband, Suresh, and her brother-in-law, Naresh. The reason for the murders, presumably, was that Kamala Devi's husband objected to her relationship with Shanta Devi. Kamala Devi and Shanta Devi dreamt of a life together, but their lives ended tragically in jail. Of course, their murder of Kamala Devi's husband Suresh—if at all they are guilty—cannot be condoned. However, what needs to be kept in mind is that the husband by objecting to Kamala Devi's affair with Shanta Devi was being oppressive. And his wife's lesbian affair cannot be treated on a par with any adulterous, extramarital heterosexual love affair, for it has to do with *preference*. When lesbians live together, the world becomes for them a sort of ideal place. The physical and psychological violence inflicted on women in a conventional marriage vanishes. There are no dominating mothers-in-law to deal with here, and the relationship is free of encumbrances like children. The lesbians are free to live for each other. This is how gender ceases to be a social construct.

Both aforementioned case studies may be said to belong to a tradition of lesbian love that was first discovered when two Kerala lesbians, Mallika, 20, and Lalithambika, 17, attempted to commit suicide. According to Ruth Vanita, "...they left behind letters stating that they could not bear imminent separation" (Vanita, 2005: 1). Lalithambika also stated in her letter that she wished to be buried with Mallika. Vanita tells us that after Mallika and Lathambika's suicide attempt, Indian newspapers began reporting a string of lesbian suicides in the years that followed. In Gujarat, two women, Jyotsna and Jayashree, threw themselves before a speeding train and ended their lives. They said in their suicide note that they could not live without each other after their parents got them married to men against their wishes. There were also a series of lesbian weddings, the most famous among these being the Hindu wedding of Leela Namdeo and Urmila Srivastava in 1998. In her analysis of lesbian suicides, Vanita tells us that it is lesbians, rather than gay men, who are most likely to commit suicide. The reasons for this are obvious. Patriarchal society gives men the right to live as they want. However, the same freedom is not given to women. This sexism was reflected in the decision of the Central Board of Film Certification (CBFC), popularly known as the Censor Board, to ban the use of the word 'lesbian'. The ban spoke volumes for the board's misogyny. The board, headed by an old (and old-fashioned) man, Pahlaj Nihalani, thought that the word 'lesbian' was a swear word. But even before Pahlaj Nihalani took over, the censor board was always known for its sexist bias. The board gave in to the Shiv Sena's demands to ban the film *Fire*, but did not ask why a similar ban was not required of the film *Bombay Boys*, which had overtly male gay characters. Obviously, the Censor Board did not go into the etymology of the word 'lesbian' before banning it. The word 'lesbian' derives from 'Lesbos', an all-woman island in ancient Greece. Today, the word 'lesbian' is political, having to do with the politics of the personal. It is not different, in that sense, from the word 'feminism'. Thus, Eve Sedgwick writes, "Feminism is the theory, lesbianism is the practice" (Sedgwick, 1990: 36). As pointed out earlier, many feminists, who are not lesbian in terms of sexual preference, nevertheless regard themselves as political lesbians. If the banning of the word 'lesbian' was triggered by moral considerations, it may be noted that, if anything, it is male homosexuals with their reputation for promiscuity that are more 'immoral' than lesbians. Lesbians, on the other hand, usually prefer stable, monogamous relationships, as the ending of *Fire* proves.

VII

Perversion

Some perverse sexual behaviors are:

- Sodomy
- Cunnilingus
- Fellatio
- Masturbation
- Rimming/Reaming
- Nudism
- Exhibitionism
- Fetishism
- S/M
- Incest
- Bestiality
- Adultery
- Pedophilia
- Voyeurism
- Group Sex
- Necrophilia

Can normativity be destabilized without a validation of perversion?

In their Preface to *Same Sex Love in India*, Vanita and Kidwai say:

> We have chosen not to use the term 'queer' favored by many scholars today because it is deemed wide enough to encompass any unconventional or strange sexual behaviors and self-constructions. For one thing, many of the behaviors and people in the texts we are dealing with are not only not represented as strange or deviant but are upheld by the texts as admirable. Second, the term 'queer' is almost too wide for our purposes, as it could include all sorts of behaviors, from fetishism to exhibitionism, which are outside the scope of our inquiry.
>
> (Vanita and Kidwai, 2000: xxi)

On the other hand, to Jonathan Dollimore, "To explore the history of perversion is to see how culture is not only formed, but consolidated, destabilized and reformed" (Dollimore, 1991: 103). Dollimore regards the history of perversion as a violent history. He says, "Perversion is a concept that takes us to the heart of a fierce dialectic between domination and deviation, law and desire, transgression and conformity; a dialectic working through repression, demonizing, displacement, and struggle" (Dollimore, 1991: 103). To him, it is the natural/ unnatural binary, which he calls one of the most fundamental of all binaries and violent of all hierarchies (since, as Derrida argues, binary opposites imply violent hierarchies) that "makes perversion and deviation conceivable, both as demonized categories, and as forms of cultural resistance" (Dollimore, 1991: 108–9). Dollimore believes that today the term 'perversion' is almost wholly understood in its sexual sense. He thus affirms that the objective is (or should be) to replace the pathological concept of perversion with a political one. Dollimore quotes Roland Barthes to whom perversion equalled liberation (Dollimore, 1991: 107). However, he cautions us against the utopian nature of the formulation when he says, "In reality, pervert nature, if only by straying, and those *in charge* will pull you in" (Dollimore, 1991: 107; emphasis mine).

Pramod K. Nayar quotes David Bell and Gill Valentine who argue that in the West, it is "only through the repetition of hegemonic heterosexual scripts" that public space becomes and remains straight. Nayar provides the example of two men kissing on a bus, calling it "an unlikely sight in India, where one does not expect to see even a heterosexist [sic] couple kissing in public." He then cites my novel *The Boyfriend* which, according to him, "presents numerous instances of how homosexuals 'queer' heterosexist space" (Bose and Bhattacharyya, 2007: 140). But Nayar's example—two men kissing on a bus—does not, in my view, amount to perverse, transgressive sex. The act of kissing (even lip kissing) does not involve the genitals, and can be taken to be the expression of affection, rather than an overt sexual act. Nayar's sheltered heterosexism has obviously not exposed him to that most perverse and transgressive of public (homo)sexual spaces in India (and elsewhere)—the gents' washroom. The range of sexual behaviors prevalent here, often in broad daylight, must be seen to be believed, for they include everything from flashing to fellatio and rimming (or reaming), to anal intercourse, to peeing on one another's body parts, etc. It is the connection here between sex and excrement, resulting in what one may call 'sexcrement', that is perverse, for while sex is associated with the pleasurable, excrement is associated with filth, which is somehow transformed into the desirable. Thus, the sight of scores of (often aroused) men defecating by the railway tracks every morning in Bombay and other metro cities may be regarded as an extension of the homosexual sexual activity that takes place in the gents' washroom. There is frontal nudity here, as the men take off their trousers (or shorts or lungis or pajamas) and face the railway tracks as they defecate, providing an unparalleled 'sexcremental' view to the thousands of commuters (of all genders) that travel on the footboard of the suburban trains, whose frequency rate is one in three minutes. (For a cinematic representation of this, see Riyad Wadia's *BomGay*, based on my poems, especially the film "Underground.")

Dollimore says, "In reality, pervert nature, if only by straying, and those in charge will pull you in" (see earlier). The gents' washroom, a perverse space, is also a hazardous space where plainclothes policemen often trap homosexuals, beat them up, and threaten to arrest them under Section 377.

In their essay "Sex in Public," Lauren Berlant and Michael Warner talk about sex as mediated by publics, and cite pornographic films, phone sex, and lap dancing as examples (During, 1999: 362). They refute Foucault's idea that bringing sexual publics into being are techniques of isolation that identify people as normal or perverse to police and pathologize them. In their view,

> In gay male culture, the principal scenes of *criminal* intimacy (emphasis mine) have been tearooms, streets, sex clubs, and parks—a tropism toward the public toilet. Promiscuity is so heavily stigmatized as non-intimate that it is often called anonymous, whether names are used or not.
>
> (During, 1999: 363)

The authors provide us with the case history of a young straight couple who confided to them that they were addicted to vibrators, sex toys, and other forms of non-reproductive eroticism. The couple told the authors: "'You are the only people we can talk to about this [addiction]; to all of our straight friends this would make us perverts.'" Responding to the statement, Berlant and Warner comment, "In order not to feel like perverts, they [the straight couple] had to make *us* into a kind of sex public" (During, 1999: 366).

The reading down of Section 377 of the IPC by the Delhi High Court in July 2009 (see Chapter IX) was not a validation of perversion. Instead, it was the validation of the normative with a caveat—though homosexuality (carnal intercourse in the language of the IPC) was still an "unnatural" offence, consenting adults who practiced it would be excluded from the provisions of the law. Homosexual lifestyle, in such a scheme of things, would become a replication of heterosexual life; thus, heteronormativity would come to be replaced by homonormativity. Homonormativists, as pointed out earlier, would argue in favor of gay marriage, which, like heterosexual marriage, would endorse the idea of the family and of private property. However, Berlant and Warner reject the term 'homonormativity'. They argue,

> Heteronormativity is ... a concept distinct from heterosexuality. One of the most conspicuous differences is that it has no parallel, unlike heterosexuality, which organizes homosexuality as its opposite. Because homosexuality can never have the invisible, tacit, society-founding rightness that heterosexuality has, it would not be possible to speak of 'homonormativity' in the same sense.
>
> (During, 1999: 355)

That the gay community was jubilant after the Delhi High Court judgment of July 2009 betrays the fact that we were moderate rather than militant or radical. While the Supreme Court judgment of December 2013 by recriminalizing homosexuality implies that it sees homosexuality as no different from other sexual perversions, the Delhi High Court judgment sought to make an exception of it. However, in excepting/accepting homosexuality, the Delhi High Court was reimagining homosexuality to mean sexual intercourse (anal, in this case) between consenting monogamous male partners. The other range of perverse possibilities that the section refers to as "unnatural" sex did not concern the learned judges. Such perverse sexual behaviors are not excluded from the provisions of Section 377 even as far as heterosexuals are concerned, let alone homosexuals. Thus, to ask a question here, would a reading down of Section 377 provide reprieve to a married man who preferred anal rather than vaginal penetrative sex with his wife? Similarly, mere heterosexuality would not come to the defense of a man who had sex with, say, a she-goat; he would be held for bestiality, regardless of the gender of the animal concerned. Speaking of bestiality, Baba Ramdev, for example, has consistently pitted it against homosexuality, indicating that both these forms of sexual activity, to him, come within the purview of the perverse. In his book *Gaysia*, Australian-Chinese author Benjamin Law quotes Baba Ramdev as saying to him, "The perversion [of homosexuality] can extend up to a level where people wish to have *sex with animals*" (emphasis original). He continues:

> It is a spectrum of perversion, from normal sexual desire to perverted sexual desire. Most male homosexuals? They are actually *heterosexual*, you know. They have their usual sexual relationships with women, but they also wish to have homosexual behavior sometimes [sic]. So it's normally an extension, a perversion of normal behavior.
>
> (Law, 2012: 285)

Though the reading down of Section 377 was no more than a sop, the gay community, hungry for social acceptance, was happy with it. For years, gay support groups in India and elsewhere have been struggling to decenter the perception that homosexuals are in search of sex and not love, and that we prefer multiple to monogamous partners. AIDS contributed towards stigmatizing promiscuity further. If, as pointed out earlier, the conspiracy theory lobbyists are to be believed, AIDS is a myth, a fake disease, foisted on the world by multinational drug cartels to find a market for their products. What probably lends credence to this view is that as a disease, AIDS has no autonomous symptoms, but relies parasitically on opportunistic infections (such as diarrhoea, tuberculosis, and pneumonia) that are said to be caused by a debilitation of the body's immunity system. But these infections also kill people who *do not* have AIDS. Still, gay support groups in India, at least since the turn of the century, have had to largely depend for their survival on AIDS-money doled out by capitalist funding agencies such as the World Health Organization (WHO). AIDS thus co-opts the gay support groups and impels them to oppose perversion. Accordingly, the gay founder of a Bombay based gay support group once reportedly beat up and dismissed an outreach worker who had sex on the premises when no one was around. The activist was worried about the 'bad name' the support group would get if the incident came to light.

In the West, AIDS became the catalyst that reinvited medical interference with homosexual lives. Foucault speaks of the "noisy entry of medicine" vis-à-vis homosexuality in 19th century Europe. At that time, homosexuality was viewed as a psychological disorder, a sickness, which could be cured by various therapies, including painful shock therapy. Benjamin Law, writing about today's China, still meets quacks in the country who attempt to "cure" their homosexual "patients" by imploring them to masturbate to pin-ups of naked women pasted on their walls, and to flagellate themselves with elastic bands whenever sinful homoerotic thoughts enter their minds. In the end, the flagellation leaves the "patients" in question with festering bruises all over their bodies, but their homosexuality does not give way to heterosexuality (Law, 2012: 99–147). Likewise, in Malaysia a Christian pastor claims he is "cured" of homosexuality by meditating to portraits of Jesus Christ and eventually marrying a woman and having children by her (Law, 2012: 185–232), while in India Baba Ramdev thinks that breathing exercises like *pranayam* are the answer to homosexuality (Law, 2012: 275–322).

As pointed out earlier, in the 20th century, the American Psychiatric Association deleted homosexuality from its list of mental disorders. But then, as the author Abraham Varghese poignantly brings out in his book *My Own Country* (1994), towards the end of the 1970s, young American homosexual men started dying (literally like flies) of this mysterious disease that would come to be called AIDS, and once again we began to witness the noisy entry of medicine in the homosexual world. In the West, AIDS was seen as a homosexual disease from the very start. Straight men and women as well as lesbians did not seem to contract it. Thus, Eve Sedgwick argues that it was AIDS that drew a wedge between homosexuals and lesbians in Europe and America after 1980. Yet, Sedgwick also says that "it remained only for the terrible accident of the HIV epidemic and the terrifyingly genocidal over-determinations of AIDS discourse to reconstruct a category of the *pervert* capacious enough to admit homosexuals of any gender" (Sedgwick, 1990: 38; emphasis mine). In India, the State being in denial mode (denying the existence of homosexuality in India), support groups like Ashok Row Kavi's Humsafar Trust had to persuade the authorities that AIDS was a gay men's disease. Before the intervention of the Humsafar Trust, the health ministry was content to view AIDS as another sexually transmitted disease (STD) that affected female sex workers, who operated from the red light districts of Indian towns and cities more than anyone else. However, that HIV infected gay men in India at least as much as it infected prostitutes is evident from the narratives in the book *An Aids Sutra* (Akhavi, 2008), a compilation of real-life AIDS stories, where the majority of contributors are gay men.

Foucault, as we have seen, asserts that gayness implies being "creative of ways of life" by altering existing lifestyles; creative, not merely in the sense of being artistic—which a lot of gay men all over the world are—but, more significantly, in the sense of being experimentalist. To me, experimentalism here would cover the whole range of perverse sexual behaviors inventoried earlier. As stated earlier, Ranjita Biswas, a lesbian feminist, interprets gay sexual experimentation here in terms of having anonymous lovers and practicing pederasty, ageism, and so on, and explains that it is such experimentation that prevents lesbians from seeing eye to eye with gay men. If anything, lesbians seem to be in favor of stability (of relationships, for one), rather than wanting to destabilize normativity through perverse sexual behavior. This, as we have seen in Chapter VI, is evidenced by the fact that the majority of homosexual women in Ashwini Sukhthankar's anthology *Facing the Mirror: Lesbian Writing from India* choose to write under a pseudonym, implying they are either closeted or selectively out, unlike the homosexual men in Hoshang Merchant's *Yaraana: Gay Writing from India* who use their real names, implying they are open about their sexuality.

The reading down of Section 377 of the IPC by Justice A. P. Shah and Justice Murlidhar of the Delhi High Court in July 2009 did not make the lesbian community as jubilant as it did the male gay community, except by way of solidarity. This is because the section, which implies that unnatural sex is unnatural *penetrative* sex, technically does not apply to women who love women. As a consequence, in Sri Lanka the government apparently came out with a supplementary law to include lesbians, which criminalized *any* form of sexual activity between people of the same sex.

As will be seen in greater detail in Chapter IX, when the Supreme Court came out with its homophobic judgment on Section 377 on December 12, 2013, there was a media outcry. Newspapers and television channels, both English and regional, slammed the judgment as retrograde. The issue went on in the media ad nauseam for the rest of the year. I was also invited to write editorial articles for three daily newspapers, *Pune Mirror* (A *Times* publication), *DNA*, and *Sakal Times* in my capacity as a gay writer and academic. In one of them, I pointed out that the way journalists had ganged up against Justice Singhvi and Justice Mukhopadhayay who gave the judgment, it was a miracle that they were not held for contempt of court, as the writer Arundhati Roy once was for adversely commenting on a Supreme Court judgment in the Sardar Sarovar Dam case.

The media hitched on to the gay rights bandwagon for its own opportunistic reasons as it wanted to come across as progressive with a 21st century mindset. It also wanted to prove, as it has always tried to, that it is a champion and guardian of human rights, and that the right to sleep with those one is sexually attracted to, and not with those whom one *is not* sexually attracted to, is a human right. In doing so, of course, it was subscribing to the contemporary view that homosexuality is natural and not cultural, related to nature rather than nurture, because it is determined by a person's chromosomal and hormonal, and ultimately genetic makeup. Some newspapers and TV channels were able to carry it off because of their left-of-centre ideologies, while others like the right-wing *Times Now* that had attacked singer Honey Singh for the "obscenity" of his lyrics, seemed self-conscious in the extreme.

But the moot point is, whether left or right wing, the newspapers and TV channels condemned the Supreme Court judgment merely in principle, assuming homosexuality to run parallel to normative heterosexuality. If any newspaper or TV channel had the slightest inkling that homosexuality equaled perversion, we can be sure that they would have instantly withdrawn their support, and in some cases, even started a tirade against us. However, as Foucault implies, unless homosexuality is equated to perversion, and is thus 'queerified', it is not putting itself to optimum use.

This chapter supports the Supreme Court judgment, albeit in an ironic way. As for the two judges, Justice Singhvi and Justice Mukhopadhayay, the less said the better. During the hearing, they are said to have made homophobic fun of the fact that author Vikram Seth's name was in the list of prominent homosexuals submitted to them by the defendants. "We love his work, but we did not know he was like *that*," they reportedly said. When given the large number of Indian men and women who are believed to be homosexual, they publicly thanked god that there were only so many of us, and no more. And they myopically concluded that a law that had been in place for nearly a hundred-and-fifty years did not have to be changed just because it affected a minuscule percentage of the population. But their English spelling was so weak that they misspelled 'minuscule' as "miniscule."

The Maoists are accused by the establishment, and by the Salwa Judum—the secret police constituted by the government to eliminate them—of thwarting development because development would be detrimental to their cause. This, however, is a distortion of the truth, which is that the Maoists reject development carried out by the State, because such development seems to them to be lopsided, merely eyewash. The lesson to be learned from this is that it is only as outlaws that we can offer real resistance conducive to a whole-scale dismantling of the status quo. The recriminalization of homosexuality by the Supreme Court pleases me because it reconfers on me the status of an outlaw, while the Delhi High Court judgment attempted to co-opt me. It is as an outlaw that I can continue my utopian fight, while as an in-law (pun intended) I am co-opted by heteronormativity.

VIII

Historiography

Lesbian-Gay-Bisexual-Transgender (LGBT) writing has existed in Indian English literature at least since independence, if not earlier. The evidence for this is present in the anthologies representing LGBT writing that have begun to make their appearance since the last decade of the 20th century. Without exception, these anthologies and critical volumes have been edited by LGBT people themselves.

As pointed out in Chapter IV, *Yaraana* was the first such anthology of gay writing to appear on the scene. It includes all the major literary genres—fiction, poetry, drama, and nonfiction—radically altering the very nature of literary compilations, which until then had been genre-specific. In addition to the English language Indian writers of repute whose work can be read in *Yaraana*, making the book a veritable Who's Who of Indian gay writing, the volume also features writing in translation from the regional languages. The prominent names here are those of Firaq Gorakhpuri (Urdu), Kamleshwar (Hindi), Namdeo Dhasal (Marathi), and Bhupen Khakar (Gujarati).

One gay poet who is conspicuous by his absence in *Yaraana* is Agha Shahid Ali. While Merchant offers no explanation in his Introduction for the exclusion of Shahid Ali from the pioneering anthology, he informally informed me that Agha Shahid Ali himself turned down an invitation to submit his work for the volume. This is because he wished to project himself as the national poet of Azad Kashmir, a position that inevitably brought him into conflict with the establishment. He did not want to further rub the establishment the wrong way, rub salt in their wounds as it were, by presenting himself as a gay poet in an anthology of gay writing, at a time when Section 377 criminalized homosexuality in the country. Besides, it is likely that conservative Kashmiri society would not accept him as the voice of Kashmir if he came out as gay. However, Merchant atones for the omission of Agha Shahid Ali in *Yaraana* by including a whole chapter on him in his critical work *Forbidden Sex/Texts* (Merchant, 2009).

In his Introduction to *Yaraana*, (Merchant, 1999: xi–xv), the author suggests that when it comes to gay writing in India, it is work in English rather than work in the regional languages that is responsible for pushing the envelope. He says, "*English speaking India* yields strident new voices like Mahesh Dattani's or R. Raj Rao's, and there are mainstream writers of *English-speaking India* like Vikram Seth, writing on gay themes" (emphasis mine).

This chapter is concerned with the censorship of queer literary history in India by mainstream literary historians. Reading Merchant's Introduction to *Yaraana*, one realizes that some of the blame for this must be put on the mass media. As pointed out earlier, Merchant says,

> In India, the MTV culture has done the country's homoerotic culture a disservice. It has projected plastic women like Sophiya Haq and Alisha Chinai onto the adolescent male imagination, depriving them of the solaces of *yaraana*. Secondly, it has projected the West's gay sub-culture in its worst light by highlighting its lunatic fringe as if it were the mainstream. Your baker, butcher, banker, bus conductor, neighbor or brother could all be very ordinary and also very gay.

Same-Sex Love in India: Readings from Literature and History (Vanita and Kidwai, 2001) is divided into four parts,

with four separate Introductions. Part I deals with ancient
Hindu India, Part II with medieval Hindu India, Part III with
medieval Islamic India, and Part IV with modern India. The
book recognizes what Foucault has called the "obscuring of
historicity" (Lotringer, 1996: 368) and attempts to set it right.
Part IV, which deals with 19th and 20th century India, includes
excerpts from six original English works. These are by Vikram
Seth and Hoshang Merchant, as well as by M. K. Gandhi, Amrita
Sher-Gil, and Inez Vere Dullas. There is also an anonymous
piece titled "Crime of Passion" summarized by the editors. The
Introduction to the section refers to Ismat Chughtai's Urdu
short story "Lihaf" (translated into English as "The Quilt") and
Kamala Das's short story "The Sandal Trees." It also refers to
(and includes an excerpt from) Vijay Tendulkar's homophobic
Marathi play *Mitrachi Goshta* (translated into English as *Mitra's
Story*), Shobha De's homophobic novel *Strange Obsession*,
mathematical wizard Shakuntala Devi's nonfiction work *The
World of Homosexuals*, and the nonfiction collection of essays
A Lotus of Another Color, edited by Rakesh Ratti. Coming to
the 1990s, the Introduction documents what it calls "positive
representations of homosexuality" in Suniti Namjoshi's fables
and poems; Nisha da Cunha's short story "La Loire Noire;"
Firdaus Kanga's autobiography *Trying to Grow*; my collection
of short stories, *One Day I Locked My Flat in Soul City*; Hoshang
Merchant's many volumes of poetry; Leslie de Noronha's
novel *Dew Drop Inn*; and P. Parivaraj's novel *Shiva and Arun*.
There is also a mention of my cycle of poems, *BomGay*, made
into an 11-minute short film by Riyad Wadia, with the same
title. Moving from full-fledged depictions of homosexual love
to books where homosexual episodes occur in the text, the
Introduction cites work by mainstream writers such as Salman
Rushdie, Hanif Kureishi, Arundhati Roy, and Vikram Chandra
whose short story "Artha" it calls a "densely imagined story."

Forbidden Sex/Texts, as its subtitle implies, is a critical
study of post-Independence India's gay poetry. Yet the book

has a section on gay theatre as well, where the work of two prominent Indian English playwrights, Mahesh Dattani and Gieve Patel, is deconstructed. While many of Dattani's plays are gay-themed, the playwright, in his anxiety to be part of the literary mainstream and not be ghettoized as a gay writer, has cleverly refrained from foregrounding gayness in his life and work. After all, a ghettoized writer is taken by the critical establishment to be an inferior artist, whose political agendas merely compensate for inadequate talent. As Merchant points out, "Dattani...could get the Sahitya Akademi award only if he did not come out as a gay in interviews." (Merchant, 2009: 76). This is also true of Gieve Patel, but as a fellow Parsi, Merchant is more charitable to him. He says, "One has to understand that Gieve Patel is a poet and poetry transcends politics" (Merchant, 2009: 77).

The real value of *Forbidden Sex/Texts* lies in its analysis of gay Indian English poetry in Section III of the book, titled "Book of the Soul." Some of the poets discussed here are Sultan Padamsee, Adil Jussawalla, Agha Shahid Ali, Vikram Seth, Suniti Namjoshi, and R. Raj Rao. A major omission from the list is Hoshang Merchant himself; obviously, Merchant could not discuss his own work in his own book.

Merchant's absolutely stellar contribution to queer Indian literary history lies in his discovery of the poetry of Sultan Padamsee (b. 1922) who committed suicide in 1945 at the young age of 23. (Merchant, 2009: 123–148). Merchant informs us that Sultan Padamsee did not publish his work in his lifetime. Instead, his book, *Poems,* came out in 1975, thirty years after his death. Merchant says,

> To begin with, it needs to be argued that Padamsee is not an Indian poet in English, especially when such a label necessitates his being viewed as a part of a tradition which has been variously addressed as Indo-Anglian to simply Indian poetry in English.

Yet, although Padamsee spent much of his short life in England, and wrote poems such as "O Pomponia Mine," "To a Lady," "Epithalamium," and "Prothalamium" which, as Merchant argues, are not necessarily 'Indian' poems, the fact is he was Indian and he was homosexual. In fact, one reason for his not publishing his poems in his lifetime, so that they had to be posthumously published after his death, could possibly be that several of them, as Merchant shows, lend themselves to queer interpretation. Merchant also makes connections between Padamsee's homosexuality and his suicide, implying that the ostensible reason for his death was his gayness. Merchant writes, "… On carefully reading his poems, one cannot but make a connection between Padamsee's homosexuality and his 'pact with death'. He took his own life, but how!"

Of the other poets whose work is discussed in *Forbidden Sex/Texts*, three have a place in the Indian English poetic canon: Adil Jussawalla, Agha Shahid Ali, and Vikram Seth. They acquire canonical status by virtue of their inclusion in the influential anthology *Twelve Modern Indian Poets* (Mehrotra, 1992) that majorly contributes to the canon-making process. However, the editorial comments on their poetry by poet–editor Arvind Krishna Mehrotra that precedes their poems does not refer to the "forbidden sex" aspect of their work at all. In Jussawalla's case, Mehrotra talks about "All the cultures that have made him invisible," (Mehrotra, 1992: 125) but that is about it. In Ali's case, it is the metaphor of exile:

> Though Ali has made exile his permanent condition, it is not what he writes about. Exile offers him unconfined and unpeopled [sic] space into which, one at a time, he introduces human figures. The eccentric and occasionally violent men of the family stand aloof from its women, who have the sensitivity of the well-born and from whom Ali inherits his own. (Mehrotra, 1992: 139)

Even Vikram Seth, who was one of the signatories to the petition to repeal Section 377, and who once admitted in a TV program on NDTV 24×7 that he was "gay or partly gay," is evaluated as a poet who parodies the grand romantic ode, and as a craftsman of "verse-making" rather than an artist. Mehrotra admits that Seth's poetry with its technical brilliance "hides the wound" but he stops short of revealing what that wound is (Mehrotra, 1992: 149).

It is left to Merchant to uncover the forbidden sex aspect of the three poets referred to here. Attempting a close reading of Jussawalla's poem "Karate," he argues that the poem "goes beyond the realm of colonialism into the sexual world as well. Jussawalla describes a kind of reverse sexual colonialism, by which a gay Indian man pursues a gay White man and kills him during sexual climax." He then concludes, "The relationship in this poem is more complicated than the typical master–slave paradigm because the two characters share a common minority as well—their homosexuality" (Merchant, 2009: 159–160).

Merchant devotes an entire chapter to Agha Shahid Ali, titled "Agha Shahid Ali's Gay Nation" (Merchant, 2009: 167–179). His central thesis in the chapter is that while as an Indian poet living in America Ali is exiled from his native Kashmir, his (homo)sexuality exiles him in a straight world. Orient-nation and orientation thus become metaphors for each other—two sides of the same coin, as it were. As evidence for Ali's gayness, Merchant cites two of his poetry collections. First, his book *The Country Without a Post Office* (the title poem here is dedicated to the gay American poet James Merrill), which has "gay subtext" and second, his book *Rooms Are Never Finished* in which he mourns his mother. Merchant's comment on the volume: "Gay poets are mother fixated though gay love is a male bonding and denotes a basic misogyny that cannot be denied." Thus, Merchant, who respects Ali's choice to stay in the closet in *Yaraana*, outs him in *Forbidden Sex/Texts*.

The title Merchant gives to his chapter on Vikram Seth is "The Anxiety of Coming Out" (Merchant, 2009: 180–204). And the title says it all. Though Seth's collections of poetry *Mappings* and *The Humble Administrator's Garden* contain a fair share of homosexual poems, which Merchant painstakingly analyzes, he is reluctant to be labeled a gay poet. This, Seth believes, will deprive him of the canonical status he aspires to, and cast him into the ghetto. *The Golden Gate*, Seth's iconic novel in verse, with its California yuppies, some of whom are gay, only reinforces this view. Merchant dissects the sonnets in *The Golden Gate* as poems, not necessarily as *gay* poems. Yet he parts with important biographical details, "He [Seth] did later share a London home with a British musician lover for 10 years, someone he dedicated *An Equal Music* (1999) to."

The chapter on Suniti Namjoshi in *Forbidden Sex/Texts* (Merchant, 2009: 205–231) is of the greatest relevance to any discussion on queer Indian literary historiography. Here, Merchant asks a set of pertinent questions and uses the work of Namjoshi to answer them. The questions are:

> Is there [a] queer contribution to literary history? Is there a continuity of queer literary tradition in India? ... Can gay and lesbian subjects who question, criticize, analyze and resist compulsory heterosexuality... contribute to liberal humanism and at the same time create a canon of their own?

And the answer is, "Suniti Namjoshi has consistently...attempted to depict queer lives as an alternative to the dominant model of history/literature, in which her modesty of moral obligations such as self-recognition and the genesis of her queer identity are persistently represented from a feminist perspective."

My work is dealt with in the same chapter as Adil Jussawalla. The chapter is subtitled, "Politics of the Avant-Garde" (Merchant, 2009: 159–166). It is in the section on *BomGay*, and in the context of the poem, that Merchant first attempts to define what may be called a queer aesthetic, different from the aesthetics of canonical literature. He writes:

> The language is explosive, shocking. The original reader reaction is that of revulsion (*bibhatsa* in the Sanskrit rasa theory) or at best derision or

mockery. The motive is to evoke a reaction to homosexuality from the complacent bourgeois.... The underlying serious intent is to shake bourgeois gentility itself. Bourgeois gentility is based on genteel language. This genteel language cloaks a lot of violence with [in] family, within social structures. By attacking this language of hypocrisy he [Rao] attacks hypocrisy itself. First appearing frivolous, he turns deadly serious, making us first uncomfortable and then marvel at his linguistic jetés!

Out: Stories from the New Queer India (Hajratwala, 2012) is published by Queer Ink, a publishing imprint founded by Shobhna Kumar, exclusively devoted to LGBT writing. The anthology showcases the work of a new generation of LGBT writers that includes names such as Gazal Dhaliwal, Dibyajyoti Sarma, Ashish Sawhny, Ashley Tellis, and several others. There is only one writer from *Yaraana*, published thirteen years before *Out*, whose work is included in the volume—me. Other established writers like Meher Pestonji appear in *Out* by virtue of their turning to gay writing for the first time. In her Introduction, editor Minal Hajratwala writes:

> Writing has been vital to the LGBT movement in India from the beginning: stapled photocopies of lesbian poems and art; protest petitions and letters to the editor; meticulous research that mines the subcontinent's rich history for proof of same-sex love in centuries past—decisively refuting the argument that *it* is a Western import. The rich and varied body of writing that has been emerging in India includes a number of earlier anthologies and studies; regional periodicals; the vast blogosphere, and a small but growing list of novels and autobiographies round out the bookshelf. The word has always been a vital element of the cause. (Hajratwala, 2012: 12–13)

It is significant to note the 'ghettoization' of LGBT writing that *Out* represents. While the mainstream publishing house Penguin Books India published both *Yaraana* and *Facing the Mirror* in 1999, no mainstream publisher has since published another anthology of LGBT writing, though in the year 2012, Penguin India reissued a slightly enlarged *Yaraana* with the subtitle *Gay Writing from South Asia*. Shobhna Kumar started Queer Ink precisely to deal with the lacuna in gay publishing.

Her inclusion of a new generation of LGBT writers in *Out* proves that the reluctance of the publishing industry to publish LGBT writing is not attributable to the fact that there are no LGBT writers today.

In the second part of my chapter, I look at three standard histories of Indian English literature, presumably by heterosexual historians, to see if the gay writers discussed above are represented in them and, if so, how.

M. K. Naik's *A History of Indian English Literature* (Naik, 1982) extensively covers the 19th and 20th centuries up to the year 1980. The work of four poets, Jussawalla, Das, Namjoshi, and Patel is referred to in a long chapter titled "The Asoka Pillar: Independence and After" (Naik, 1982: 187–283). While Naik cites a poem from Jussawalla's *Missing Person*, with its lines "a gigantic Shiva thrust" and a "Black and Decker drill," his prudishness and his cultural naiveté prevent him from commenting on the obvious phallic implications of this and other poems. Kamala Das' poetry is pejoratively described as a "generally sex dominated poetry" that forecloses all possibility of seeing the personal as the political, which is so crucial to Das' work. Namjoshi's radical lesbian-feminism eludes Naik, and all he is able to do is compare her to Sarojini Naidu with whom she has little in common. While Naik refers to Patel's play *Princes*, he would not be in a position to comment on *Mister Behram*, Patel's play with a queer subtext, as it was written after the publication of Naik's book. However, even if that were not the case, one is certain that Naik, a Brahmanical critic and literary historian, would be silent on the play's homoeroticism.

Bruce King's *Modern Indian Poetry in English* (2001) has sections on Jussawalla, Das, Patel, Seth, Ali, Merchant, Namjoshi, and me. The critique on Jussawalla (King, 2001: 244–251), shows that King has painstakingly sifted through all his poems, especially in *Missing Person*. Yet, King beats around the bush and does not take the bull by the horns.

He speaks of Jussawalla's preoccupation with alienation, and attributes it to his "not being part of the society in which he lives...." But what is the alienation due to? Surely, sexuality has a role to play here, but King is silent on the subject. Sexuality may occupy a relatively minor place in Jussawalla's "increased radical social awareness," in the politicization of his poetry, and in his identification "with a revolutionary process in which the peoples of the Third World will create a new society." But he understands it as a category, just as race and class are categories. It is this understanding that prompts Merchant to include him in his selections in *Yaraana* and his chapters in *Forbidden Sex/Texts*. Ironically, King as an American critic and historian fails to see Jussawalla as a part of a larger coalition.

King sees the life and writing of Kamala Das (King, 2001: 147–154) in chiefly heterosexist ways. Expressions such as "sexual partner," "sexuality," "free love," "sexual passions," "feelings of intimacy," "sexually driven," "act of sex," and "feelings of love" abound in the section on her. And though he says that she (Das) "describes a void to be filled with others or with *alternative* passions" (emphasis mine), he does not spell out what those alternative passions are. Instead, he says:

> There is...her obsession with an older *man* who 'hurt' her in her teens and whom she obsessively feels she must capture as her lover.... While the poems describe a longing for a *man* to fill her dreams with love, she is also proud of her conquests and ability to make *men* love her (emphasis mine).

What King does not say is that the *alternative* passions Das describes have to do with her turning to women for pleasure and intimacy when she fails to find these in the oppressive world of men. Love, for Kamala Das, is always gender-neutral, never gender-specific.

The one sexual analogy King detects in Patel, seemingly leads him to the conclusion that it is heterosexual. The poem in question is "The Arrogant Meditation" and the lines are "Trees/Push their way upward" and "Grovelling underground/ Tubers acquire volume" (King, 2001: 119). But I would argue that the mere use of tubers acquiring volume, which obviously is a metaphor for pregnancy, does not in itself imply heterosexuality, for the poem also talks about trees pushing their way upward, which is a metaphor for potency. Thus, the poet perceives both pregnancy and potency at the same time, hinting at a sort of bisexuality (the 'B' in the LGBT formulation).

It is in the section on Vikram Seth (King, 2001: 226–230) that King is finally able to connect discord with one's father, anti-romanticism, loneliness, a sense of being continually on the move, and loving strangers, to homosexuality and bisexuality, so evident in Seth's work. However, there is still a homophobic unwillingness on his part to make these connections on his own. Instead, he wants Seth to make them for him, as the following sentence implies, "While his [Seth's] feeling of marginality is furthered by *his* declared bisexuality, it is also the typical perspective of the alien in a foreign society…" (emphasis mine).

The most clinching instance of the censorship of queer Indian historiography is provided by Bruce King's chapter on Agha Shahid Ali, titled "The Diaspora: Agha Shahid Ali's Tricultural Nostalgia" (King, 2001: 257–274). Here, King offers us a nearly 20-page volume by volume analysis of Ali's poetry. However, the analysis is entirely from the point of view of the diaspora, childhood, exile, nostalgia, independence, postcolonialism, postmodernism, language, culture, Kashmir, Islam, and America. There is no mention whatsoever of Ali's homosexuality. Even when King refers to Ali's 'longings' the longings are for a place (Kashmir) rather than for a person. Likewise, his "fantasies about roads not taken" are not homosexual fantasies. King refers to Ali's "re-categorization" as an Indian English poet in Mehrotra's *Twelve Modern Indian Poets*. But why doesn't he comment on Ali's exclusion as a gay poet from Merchant's *Yaraana* which appeared two years before King's own book?

The last three poets, Merchant, Namjoshi, and me, figure in the chapter titled "New Poets, Styles and Feelings" (King, 2001: 333–354). A single paragraph links the three poets, as well as Vikram Seth. King writes:

> Homosexuality is a theme of Hoshang Merchant's...many volumes [of poetry], as it sometimes is in the writings of R. Raj Rao. Vikram Seth has at times alluded to it. I am not aware of much Indian poetry in English that treats lesbianism. Perhaps the publications have not come to my attention. Suniti Namjoshi published with Writers Workshop... but only became more widely known after her openly lesbian short stories and fables were published in England.... (emphasis mine)

A few paragraphs later, King says, "Rao's mixture of Swiftian satire and gay activism is unsettling and meant to be."

The first edition of *Modern Indian Poetry in English* came out in 1987, 14 years before the edition discussed in this chapter. None of India's more openly gay poets (except Vikram Seth) were covered in the first edition. During his 14-year exile, in the manner of Lord Ram of the Ramayana, King seems to have acquired enough political correctness to be able to use the words gay, lesbian, and homosexual in his "New Poets" chapter, which was not a part of the first edition. However, his claim that "the [lesbian] publications have not come to my attention" in the passage quoted earlier must continue to intrigue us. King's research is otherwise meticulous. Why was he unable to see the strands of lesbianism not just in the poetry of Namjoshi, but more significantly in the poetry of Kamala Das? Was the resistance on account of homophobia?

Indian English Literature 1980–2000 (Naik and Narayan, 2011) was intended as a sequel to *A History of Indian English Literature*. Its aim was to cover the last twenty years of the 20th century. M. K. Naik teams up with another professor–historian, Shyamala A. Narayan here. Of the most overtly gay writers discussed in the book, the authors do maximum justice to Mahesh Dattani (Naik and Narayan, 2011: 206–209). They call the homosexuality depicted in Dattani's plays "an explosive subject (for an Indian)" and say that "Dattani is the first Indian English playwright of note to deal with this theme." (They contradict themselves a few pages later when they talk about my play *The Wisest Fool on Earth* as a play in which the protagonist "waxes eloquent over the privileges and pleasures of being a homosexual.") For the first time, Naik and Narayan speak of a "motif of homosexuality" that binds Dattani's plays such as *Bravely Fought the Queen* and *A Muggy Night in Mumbai*, especially the latter. They talk about the play presenting "a group of well-to-do homosexuals in Bombay, their changing mutual relationships, their revelations, their self-delusions and self-discoveries." The authors also praise the play *Seven Steps Around the Fire* "for offering many insights into the lives of the *hijras*, and their beliefs and customs."

The other gay writers are spoken of somewhat dismissively. Though the authors say of my work that it "boldly celebrates homosexuality" and that "this brave attempt to widen the thematic horizons of the short story is certainly commendable," they also say, "one wonders whether the writer has been fully successful in conveying to us the essence of the homosexual experience, the distinctive way in which it differs from *normal* love, and its psychological and other repercussions" (Naik and Narayan, 2011: 127; emphasis mine). An almost identical thing is said about Merchant. Speaking of his many volumes of homosexual poetry, the authors say, "…one is not sure how far he [Merchant] has succeeded in showing how exactly, and in what particular respects, this experience differs from that of love of the *normal* variety" (Naik and Narayan, 2011: 175; emphasis mine).

The reference to heterosexual love as "normal," and, by implication, homosexual love as "abnormal," smacks of homophobia. Naik and Narayan thus succeed in 'othering' the homosexual writer. They fail to understand that the whole point of gay writing is to show that homosexual love is *not* different from other types of love.

Besides the above writers, the only other writer whose homosexual writing is alluded to is Firdaus Kanga. Once again, the writers speak of Kanga's aspirations in his books to live in Britain, "where he can aspire to lead a *normal* life in spite of his osteoporosis and his homosexual *inclinations...*" (Naik and Narayan, 2011: 222; emphasis mine). To call homosexuality an 'inclination' or a 'tendency' as opposed to a 'preference' again smacks of homophobia.

There is merely a veiled reference to Suniti Namjoshi's lesbianism in the remark, "Her fables are even more effective than her poems in speaking up for the rights of the marginalized" (Naik and Narayan, 2011: 138). Vikram Seth fares even more badly. His poems in *The Humble Administrator's Garden* are not acknowledged for their homosexual content, but because the poet effectively "describes the boiling over of soup on the stove." The authors then quote his line "to make love with a stranger is the best" (Naik and Narayan, 2011: 172–173), but the homosexual undertones of the line are lost on them.

The censorship of queer literary history in India shows no signs of abating. In *The Cambridge History of Indian Poetry in English* edited by Rosinka Chaudhuri (2016) there are no essays on the poetry of Hoshang Merchant, Suniti Namjoshi, and me, though I have an essay in the book on the poetry of Kamala Das and Eunice de Souza, in which I analyze lesbian interpretations of Das' poems. LGBT writing, it appears, will have to write its own history just as it must create its own aesthetics.

IX

The Politics of Section 377, IPC

On October 6, 1860, the Indian Law Commission, presided over by Lord T. B. Macaulay, introduced Section 377 of the Indian Penal Code. The section was worded as follows:

> Whoever voluntarily has carnal intercourse against the order of nature with any man, woman or animal, shall be punished with imprisonment for life, or with imprisonment of either description for a term which may extend to ten years, and shall also be liable to fine.

Explanation: Penetration is sufficient to constitute the carnal intercourse necessary to the offence described in this Section.

Comment: This Section is intended to punish the offence of sodomy, buggery, and bestiality. The offence consists in a carnal knowledge committed against the order of nature by a person with a man, or in the same unnatural manner with a woman, or by a man or woman in any manner with an animal.

While Section 377 covers all forms of non-heterosexual and non-procreative sexual activity, the representation of such activity in literature may be said to be covered by the Section only by default. Though Section 377 received a temporary reprieve between July 2009 and December 2013, when the

Delhi High Court ruled that it would not apply to consensual sex by LGBT people above the age of 18, it was revived by the Supreme Court in December 2013, when it set aside the earlier Delhi High Court judgment.

In December 2013, homosexuality was recriminalized in India. By afternoon that day, news of the judgment had spread all over the country, and indeed all over the world. The gay community suddenly felt insecure again and decided to cling together for solidarity. Every news channel on television, regardless of what language they aired their programmes in, had managed to bring gay activists and lawyers together to conduct live discussions on the judgment. The judgment, to say the least, was entirely unexpected. Justice A. P. Shah's Delhi High Court verdict of July 2009, which had read down Section 377 of the IPC, had been challenged in the Supreme Court by, among others, yoga guru Baba Ramdev. But we sincerely believed that, at the end of the day, the Supreme Court would uphold the Delhi High Court ruling. When some of us wondered why the Supreme Court took so long to deliver its judgment subsequent to the appeal, lawyers explained that the Supreme Court was merely being cautious as it had to keep the interests of all and sundry, including the fanatics, in mind.

When the judgment was out, it belied everyone's hopes. We felt claustrophobic, unable to see any light at the end of a very long and dark tunnel. After all, apex court judgments are sacro-sanct and not easily reversible. Nor was the union government going to amend the law itself and get rid of Section 377.

Life goes on. Law or no law, judgment or no judgment, people will be what they are and no earthly power can change that. Additional Solicitor General Indira Jaisingh said in a television programme that judges should not let their personal prejudices interfere with their judgments. Unfortunately, that is what happened in this case.

Then came the general elections of May 2014. While mainstream India rejoiced over the election results and the formation of the new government, the verdict did not augur well with the queer community (see discussion later). We were full of apprehension. Would we be treated on a par with other social and political criminals? Would there be witch-hunting to get us, as in some African countries like Uganda?

When the Supreme Court upturned the Delhi High Court ruling of July 2009, it put the onus on the union government, saying it was for the government to amend the existing law, if it thought fit. That, of course, would depend on which government was in power. From the way Sonia Gandhi and Rahul Gandhi reacted to the judgment, making it clear they were outraged by it because it was an intrusion of a person's privacy, we assumed that the Congress, if it came to power, would initiate steps to change the law. Later, Arvind Kejriwal's Aam Aadmi Party (AAP) also held meetings with queer activists, reiterating that they were appalled by the judgment, and would do everything they could to restore the fundamental rights of gay people. That is why, the 'wave' notwithstanding, most gay men and lesbians voted for the Congress and the AAP.

The Bharatiya Janata Party (BJP), however, was jubilant about the judgment from the very start. It supported it fully, which meant that it would do nothing to introduce a parliamentary amendment that would lead to the scrapping of Section 377. It was obvious why the BJP took such a stand. As a Hindu nationalist party, it believed it had to safeguard Indian culture and Indian values, and homosexuality, according to it, was against Indian culture. The people of India did not want it. According to the BJP, homosexuality was a Western fad that touched the lives of a few phony upper-class Indians, while middle-class India was completely unaffected by it. What middle-class India knew was heterosexuality, marriage, procreation, and the starting of family—made up of father, mother, brother, and sister. And Section 377 of the IPC endorsed all that.

But that brings me to the other worrying thing—the thing about minorities. The party that won the mandate of the janta is known to be myopic about the existence of minorities. Their hostility toward religious minorities, especially Muslims, is legion. If they believed that homosexuals were also a minority, it meant that we were invisible to our government, we did not exist for them, and we were our country's lost property.

When the Supreme Court delivered its judgment on Section 377 in December 2013, it capitalized on the word 'minority'. It suggested that a law that was in place for 143 years did not have to be changed to suit the whims and fancies of a "minuscule" minority. It was as if the judiciary was colluding with the legislature here to blot out the presence of minorities. That left only the executive, the babus of babuland, the police included, who were not exactly known to be the best friends of gay folk.

The election results veritably pushed the gay community against a wall. First, the December 2013 judgment was not in our favour. Then, a review petition that was filed to reconsider the December 2013 judgment was dismissed by the Supreme Court. A curative petition that was subsequently filed to review the December 2013 judgment again (this time by a five-judge bench), showed no signs of coming up. And now, a political party that was vociferously opposed to legitimizing non-heterosexual sex got a thumping majority in Parliament.

A year after the December 2013 judgment, members of India's LGBT community gathered in Delhi to condemn the Supreme Court's recriminalization of homosexuality. Eminent people from the gay and transgender communities such as documentary filmmaker Sridhar Rangayan and activist Laxmi (Laxminarayan Tripathi) flew to Delhi all the way from Bombay to participate in the event. No less a luminary than Mr K. G. Balakrishnan, Chairman of the National Human Rights Commission of India and a former Chief Justice, spoke at the event. Mr Balakrishnan said, "Human rights of the LGBT community need protection, and they should not be classified as criminals." I too was in Delhi at the time to participate in a documentary film conference titled *Visible Evidence*, where I took part in a workshop on the topic "LGBTQ Documentary in India After 377: Where are We Coming from, Where are We Going."

An NGO called SPACE (Society for People's Awareness, Care and Empowerment) conducted an independent study of the scene in India after the December 2013 judgment. Their findings were shocking. They discovered that within the first three months of the judgment, a gay man and three transgender persons were brutally murdered in different parts of the country because of their sexual orientation. Respondents interviewed by SPACE pointed out that though they faced homophobic violence both inside and outside the home, they were apprehensive about reporting the matter to the police. They felt that the police would arrest them, rather than the perpetrators of the violence, since it was they who were supposed to be 'criminals'. Interviewees also talked of being thrown out of housing societies by their landlords soon after the judgment, for the landlords knew or suspected that they were gay. Others said they did not have the same easy access to condoms as before, which implied they were being denied the right to safe sex. Those who were stricken with AIDS decided not to avail of the antiretroviral therapies (ART) provided at government hospitals, because that could trap them and lead to their arrest.

The tales recounted, to the volunteers of SPACE as well as at the meeting in Delhi, were heartbreaking. Rudrani Chettri, a transgender activist like Laxmi, spoke of how police constables thrashed her with their batons as she celebrated New Year's Eve in Shimla. They beat her up not because she was ushering in the New Year—which everyone does—but because they wanted to molest her, and she resisted their advances.

Post-December 2013, mainstream society joined hands with the law to oppress the LGBT community. Khush Mishra, a homosexual man with a girlfriend, narrated a strange saga. His girlfriend borrowed the money he was saving for himself (close to a lakh rupees) to have a sex-change operation. But when he asked her to return the money, she did not. The reason? She did not want him to have the sex reassignment surgery, so that he would continue to be her boyfriend. But the matter got messy, with Khush complaining to the girl's father about the money lent to his daughter, and the father, instead of asking his daughter to return the money, complaining to the police. The police, of course, entirely relied on the father's side of the story, which made out his daughter to be a victim. The police beat up and arrested Khush. He became an all-round loser, having lost his money, his girlfriend, his freedom, and the means to have his sex-change operation.

The December 2013 judgment made LGBT people vulnerable. Perhaps, it would have been better had the Delhi High Court not read down Section 377 in July 2009. That judgment, as it turned out, was a deception. It led us to believe that we were liberated. In truth, however, we were caught between the devil and the deep blue sea.

A 92-minute film titled *No Easy Walk to Freedom*, directed by Nancy Nicol, effectively captured how we felt. It chronicled India's gay liberation struggle since the time the Naz Foundation of Delhi filed a petition in the Delhi High Court to amend Section 377. The fight was by no means easy. At first, the court dismissed the petition as irrelevant. However, the perseverance of the petitioners, several of them such as Anjali Gopalan, Anand Grover, and Gautam Bhan belonging to a syndicate known as the Lawyers' Collective, compelled the court to revisit the case and ask the Government of India for its take (and stake) in the matter. The film documented how the petitioners scored a point when the government found itself in a spot—one of its ministries, the Ministry of Health, seeing merit in the petition, even as another ministry, the Home Ministry, argued that homosexuality was against Indian culture. The film conducted a detailed interview with queer historian Saleem

Kidwai, one of the authors of the book *Same Sex Love in India*, referred to earlier. Kidwai explained that homosexual love was known and practiced in precolonial India, both in the ancient and medieval period. It is the English Victorians who outlawed it in England, India, and in all their other colonies all over the world. So, to say that homosexuality is against Indian culture is incorrect. To prove Kidwai's point, the film offers close shots of the temple sculptures in Khajuraho, Madhya Pradesh. The Khajuraho temples were built by the Chandelas in the 4th century AD The sculpture on the temple walls depicts group sex involving both heterosexuals and homosexuals, proving that sexual orientation is fluid.

No Easy Walk to Freedom opens to scenes of dancing, singing, and the lighting of firecrackers all over India as Justice A. P. Shah's Delhi High Court judgment of July 2009 that read down Section 377, excluding consenting adult homosexuals from its purview, is out. Justice Shah himself appears in the film and explains the difference between constitutional morality and morality in general, which prompted his decision. According to him, what the term 'constitutional morality' implied in the present case was that while homosexuality seemed immoral to conservative society, to outlaw it would be to deny a group of citizens their fundamental rights, guaranteed to them by the Constitution of India, even if, as in this case, they constituted a microscopic minority. The film documented how homophobia in India was on the decline in the aftermath of the July 2009 judgment. More gay and trans-people felt emboldened to come out, and their families were more willing to accept them as compared to before. However, after the Supreme Court reversed the Delhi High Court judgment four-and-a-half years later, the gay community felt susceptible all over again. Many of them had made their sexual orientation known to the world in the light of the Delhi High Court judgment, and now there was no knowing who would persecute them, and where, and when.

The Supreme Court judgment notwithstanding, Nancy Nicol did not let her film end on a pessimistic note. Both queer and nonqueer people come together in the film to continue the fight. Well-known gay activists who appeared in the film to express their solidarity included Ashok Row Kavi of the Humsafar Trust, Bombay; Shobhna Kumar of Queer Ink, Bombay; Manohar of Sangama, Bangalore; and Arvind Narrain, who co-edited the book *Because I Have a Voice* with Gautam Bhan (Narrain and Bhan, 2005). The film ended with Gautam Bhan addressing a rally in Delhi. He was so animated in his speech and gestures, pledging that he would fight to the finish no matter what, that I was instantly reminded of America's Harvey Milk, who fought for gay rights in America in the 1960s and 1970s.

Ten months after the Supreme Court judgment, actor Aamir Khan did a programme on homosexuality in his television series *Satyamev Jayate*. Openly gay and transgender people such as Deepak Kashyap and Gazal Dhaliwal participated in the show. It was a risky thing to do, considering that the judgment had rendered all LGBT people criminals, technically at least. In order to make Aamir Khan understand how gay people felt, psychologist Anjali Chabria, present on the show, asked him if it would be possible for him to sleep with another man. The point she was trying to make was just as Aamir Khan, a self-identified heterosexual, could not sleep with another man, self-identified LGBT people could not sleep with persons of the opposite sex. However, to me, Aamir Khan's vehement and aggressive refusal when asked if he could sleep with another man, smacked of homophobia. There was no need for him to be so much on the defensive. Yet, Aamir Khan needed to be congratulated for airing the show in brazen defiance of the law. He also had to be complemented for including not just LGBT people themselves in the programme, but also their family members including their parents, who supported their children and said they would stand by them at all costs.

Both Gautam Bhan and Anjali Gopalan, who had earlier appeared in *No Easy Walk to Freedom*, reappeared in the Aamir Khan programme. Bhan pointed out, significantly, that the wording of Section 377 of the IPC was itself flawed. It foreclosed the possibility of change, because it had already made up its mind that homosexuality was "unnatural." Thus, a mere reading down of Section 377 was not going to be of help. What was required was a full-scale abolition of the archaic law. In a follow-up to the *Satyamev Jayate* show, known as *Mumkin Hai*, Aamir Khan invited viewers to tweet their views on Section 377. Apparently, he received over sixteen thousand tweets calling for the scrapping of Section 377.

In April 2014, the Supreme Court recognized transgender people as the third gender, neither male nor female. The judgment ran contradictory to the December 2013 judgment. For, transgender people are rarely heterosexual. The conflict between their biological and psychological identities ensures that they are sexually attracted to people of their own sex. A transgender male, for example, feels he is a woman partly because he is attracted to men. In April 2014, the Supreme Court held that transgender people deserved the same rights as others. Thus, it recommended reservations for them in educational institutions and government jobs. The new Supreme Court judgment implied that transgender people were excluded from the provisions of Section 377. Taken to its logical conclusion, it meant that if a gay man had "unnatural" sex with a transgender male, the gay man alone would be punished. It was a Catch 22 situation. If the Supreme Court upheld transgender rights, but continued to criminalize (or at least remain silent) about their sexual behavior, it implied that transgender people must remain celibate for the rest of their lives!

Ideally, the two cases, the appeal against the Delhi High Court ruling that read down Section 377 and the Public

Interest Litigation (PIL) filed by the NGO Alliance India for transgender rights, should have been heard together in the Supreme Court. However, the two cases were heard by two separate benches. The hands of the latter bench, comprising Justice K. S. Radhakrishnan and Justice A. K. Sikri, were obviously tied. They could not embarrass the Supreme Court by going against its own December 2013 judgment. Hence, they made it clear that while dealing with the present issue they were not concerned with this aforesaid wider meaning of the expression 'transgender'. The "aforesaid wider meaning" had of course to do with the clubbing of 'lesbian', 'gay', and 'bisexual' with the term 'transgender'. This was commented upon by Supreme Court advocate Raju Ramachandran in an op-ed page article in *The Indian Express*. Ramachandran was an advocate for the petitioners in the transgender rights case. He wrote, "In the gay rights case, the Delhi High Court had taken the view that discrimination on grounds of sexual orientation was discrimination on the grounds of sex. Unfortunately, the Supreme Court did not even touch upon this aspect in its December [2013] judgment." In the concluding paragraph of his article, Ramachandran said,

> One court, two mindsets. The lesson that we need to learn is this: constitutional adjudication is serious business. Article 145(3) requires that a minimum number of five judges sit to decide any substantial question of law relating to the interpretation of the Constitution. The court ought to do this strictly. (Ramachandran, April 18, 2014: 9)

The April 2014 judgment also implied that the law now had a serious loophole. How would it prove whether one was a transgender or not? Castration was a criterion, but then as Laxmi told author Salman Rushdie, "Only about 60 percent of Bombay hijras actually have the operation, although, they say, in Gujarat it is insisted upon" (Akhavi, 2008: 111). Homosexual men, often naturally effeminate, could take advantage of the law by claiming to be transgender. All it would take on their part is to cross-dress, wear jewelry, and cultivate habitual feminine body language. As for job reservations, the judgment could open up a Pandora's Box. 'Transgender' is a psychological state, difficult to prove by clinical means. Sexual orientation, being biological, is relatively easier to prove. Homosexual and heterosexual men alike could feign transgender behavior and apply for jobs under the transgender quota.

Then the Government of India did what we expected it to do. It challenged the Supreme Court's April 2014 judgment on transgender rights, proving in the bargain that it did not respect judicial independence. It seemed as if the attorney general had not even bothered to read the April 2014 judgment carefully. Thus, one of his contentions was that lesbian, gay, and bisexual identities had to be delinked from transgender identities. As pointed out earlier, the Supreme Court was obliged to do this, because it could not contradict its own judgment of December 2013 that recriminalized homosexuality. The bench that gave the April 2014 judgment was apparently of a progressive mindset, unlike the bench that gave the December 2013 judgment. The former bench cleverly found a loophole in the law when it upheld transgender rights, because, as explained earlier, in the formulation L, G, B, and T, the T alone has to do with gender identity, while the other letters represent sexual preference.

The government erred when it assumed that 'transgender' was an umbrella term that also covered lesbian, gay, and bisexual identities. However, there are overlaps between 'transgender' on the one hand, and 'lesbian', 'gay', and 'bisexual' on the other, which make the April 2014 judgment somewhat untenable. If a transgendered person is also gay, it is ridiculous to suggest that the former person in him has rights, while the latter does not.

As to the business of giving Other Backward Class (OBC) status to transgender people, which would entitle them to government jobs through the quota system, the government took exception to this, bringing in a technicality. OBC status, it claimed, could not be given to transgenders, in spite of the Supreme Court ruling, because that would have to be first okayed by the National Commission for Backward Classes (NCBC). Needless to say, the NCBC was not going to okay it. In India, the hijras are the most visible face of transgendered people. The only work they are able to find is begging, singing, dancing, and sex work, all for a pittance. Reserving government jobs for them, if it could be properly monitored, would perhaps enable them to lead dignified lives. But was the government really concerned about their dignity?

The BJP was effectively the only political party that lauded the December 2013 judgment. When the judgment came out, of course, the BJP was still not in power at the centre. Five months later it came to power, and disregarded the independence of the judiciary by asserting that it would constitute its own panel to adjudicate on the matter and would strictly go by its recommendations. The media advised the BJP government to amend Section 377, even if it meant losing the support of its conservative, right-wing voters. The BJP ignored this advice.

The judgment emboldened men with a right-wing mindset. Some of them trivialized the issue. One such gentleman, a Delhi based advocate, filed a case in a metropolitan court in Delhi, arguing that if Section 377 criminalized homosexuality, then it was incumbent upon the government to ban the use of "sex toys" that were meant to stimulate "unnatural" sexual activity. The advocate in question went as far as to name the firms that manufactured these products, which could be bought online. Instead of dismissing the absurd petition, the metropolitan magistrate attached to the concerned court admitted it. The PIL, strange as it was, put the court in a quandary. Hence, they threw the ball into the police's court, asking the latter to investigate the advocate's allegations. The cops' brief was to file an "action taken report" on whether the sale of anal lube, desensitizer, and spray—items named in the advocate's complaint—abetted acts that Section 377 made illegal. The fact that the metropolitan court admitted the petition was alarming. It meant that in the future, similar petitions could be filed against queer art, queer literature, and queer cinema. After all, they too violated the provisions of Section 377 through representative acts.

Section 377 criminalized certain kinds of sexual activity. How could it be proved that the sale of "sex toys" inevitably led to "unnatural" sexual activity per se? At the most, it could be argued that the items had the *potential* to stimulate sexual activity. But then, so did the food we ate. Could a ban be imposed on the sale of onions and cloves on the grounds that they stimulated anal sex?

When questioned about the relevance of his petition, the advocate claimed that he was merely "testing the law." He unconvincingly resorted to political correctness by saying, "My complaint is not against the LGBT community. It is against the unreasonableness of Section 377, which seeks to regulate the basic privacy of people and wants law enforcement to act as an unrelenting Peeping Tom."

The advocate's statement smacked of hypocrisy. All of us were against the unreasonableness of Section 377. But we did not employ reactionary and roundabout methods, such as those employed by him, to get rid of it. If the advocate was serious about the repealing of Section 377, there were many avenues in Delhi, where he lived, that were open to him. He could join the Lawyers' Collective, or the Naz Foundation, or Voices Against 377—all of which were involved in the fight against Section 377. There was no need for him to jeopardize the welfare of the LGBT community, which was already in the doldrums, by playing monitor. To me, his PIL was tantamount to his saying in schoolboy fashion, "Sir, look what the LGBT community is doing. It is playing with sex toys."

The advocate dishonestly spoke of Section 377 regulating the privacy of people, pretending to be on the side of the LGBT community. Months later, a debate on the right to privacy trended on the national media. It was triggered by an incident in Bombay where the police broke into a flat where a group of youngsters were partying. The question was should the right to privacy be regarded as a fundamental right. The conservative position was that the right to privacy could not be a fundamental right because it would result in anarchy. If everyone did exactly as they pleased, even within the confines of their homes, they would find themselves in conflict with the law. To such people, things like premarital sex, adulterous sex, and group sex, even if practiced within the four walls of a house, could topple society's stable foundations. To the proponents of the conservative view, the word 'privacy' meant virtually nothing. It was a licentious word that was best abolished once and for all, for it had associations of sinful behavior where morals were jettisoned. The conservative faction thus took on the role of moral custodians. Their wisdom was received wisdom that they heard for generations together from parents, grandparents, and great grandparents. What they mouthed were platitudes. One of them, referring to the Bombay incident that triggered the debate, asked on TV if the parents of the youngsters knew what they were up to at the party. To which a youngster participating in the show retorted that since she was above the age of 18, she did not have to ask her parents for permission to have sex!

The liberals were slightly better. But they too wanted the line to be drawn somewhere. The anchor of the TV show belonged to this category. He tied himself up in knots when he conceded with a conservative panelist that privacy did not mean that one could assemble a bomb in one's house. Moreover, the TV anchor was formulating the idea of privacy in terms of heterosexual sex. He defended sex outside marriage, but wrongly assumed that this, invariably, was heterosexual sex. The anchor did not refer to homosexuality even once. Homosexual sex could not be brought within the purview of the right to privacy, because the law of the land declared it to be illegal. A homosexual was thus no different from an anarchist.

The term 'anarchist' has been applied to Arvind Kejriwal. In February 2015, Kejriwal's Aam Aadmi Party came to power in Delhi with a thumping majority. This was good news for the LGBT community. After the December 2013 judgment, the Aam Aadmi Party was one of the few parties that took a stand on Section 377. Many of the Aam Aadmi Party's key members were lawyers by profession, and they looked at the matter from a legal perspective. They spoke of a legal amendment that would get rid of the 1860 law once and for all. But for that they would have to acquire power at the centre. Still, the views of the Aam Aadmi Party's (then) more prominent members, such as Yogendra Yadav and Prashant Bhushan, not to speak of Kejriwal himself, indicated that they were not blind to the predicament of minorities, regardless of who those minorities were. Prashant Bhushan was once even beaten up in his office by lumpen elements belonging to the right wing, just because he spoke up for Kashmir's minorities. Yogendra Yadav described the BJP as 'majoritarian'. Did that imply that the Aam Aadmi Party was 'minoritarian'?

India's sexual minorities were as much of the *aam aadmi* or common man as anyone else, though, to the best of my knowledge, well-known cartoonist R. K. Laxman never once depicted us in his common man cartoons. Yet, we were the subaltern, not the elite—the proletariat, not the bourgeoisie. The majority of LGBT people faced discrimination at home, at the workplace, and in their neighborhoods. They were frequently laughed and scoffed at. But they had no option but to quietly go about their lives. Moreover, even if a section of LGBT people in India were affluent and Westernized, affluence and Westernization were not a barrier against homophobia.

US President Barak Obama visited India for a much-hyped meeting with Prime Minister Narendra Modi. However, no mention was made by him of India's retrograde anti-gay law. This was unfortunate considering that, soon after the December 2013 judgment, President Obama appeared on US television to condemn the Supreme Court judgment as a violation of human rights. However, many months later, when there was actually a chance for him to discuss the issue with Prime Minister Modi, he seemed to have forgotten all about it. Indeed, the subject of human rights seemed to be nowhere on the two leaders' agenda. It is possible that the Indian government does not see the rights of sexual minorities as a part of human rights. It is here that the Americans could have stepped in to expand and broaden the scope and definition of human rights for us, so as to fit in with their own way of thinking. In the US, more and more states have begun to legalize gay marriage.

Let alone the US President, even members of the Indian diaspora in America, who flocked at the sight of Prime Minister Modi at Madison Square when he visited the country, did not touch on the subject. America's Indian community is made up of a large number of LGBT people. They even have their support groups like SALGA (South Asian Lesbian and Gay Association) and their own newsletters like *Trikone*. The least they could have done for us is to hand Prime Minister Modi a letter expressing regret at the restoration of Section 377. The Indian law, of course, does not affect the diaspora directly. But it affects them indirectly, as the narratives in the book *A Lotus of Another Color* (referred to earlier) show. Here, many lesbian and gay Americans of Indian origin (some of them are second-generation immigrants) provide testimonies of their dilemma. While their sexual orientation drives them toward gay lifestyles, their families forever send them on guilt trips for spurning Indian culture and Indian values, and allowing American ideas to 'corrupt' them. In any case, the criminalization of something—anything—has a damaging psychological effect on human beings. Once it ceases to be a crime, people's prejudices disappear.

When the US Supreme Court legalized homosexuality and gay marriage all over America a few months later, an optimistic section of the Indian media urged the government to emulate America's example and abolish Section 377. However, as pointed out earlier, it seemed well nigh impossible that the BJP government, given its right-wing ideology, would heed that advice. The government seemed much more prone to listening to the advice of holy men like Baba Ramdev, and many others, who have called homosexuality unnatural and perverse. Some of them have also made the bogus claim that homosexuality can be 'cured'. The BJP government looks toward America when it comes to mimicking their capitalist model, earning Prime Minister Narendra Modi the epithet of *suit-boot ki sarkar* by the opposition. However, it will go all out to contest their liberal approach to homosexuality. The government continues to revel in its ill-informed view that homosexuality has been foisted on India by the West, and only Westernized, upper-class Indians call themselves gay. Middle-class India, according to our politicians, is one hundred percent straight, and that is why we have so many marriages and so many children in India. But the truth is that in middle-class India, many men and women who get married are actually gay, and perhaps they would not have got married if the law was less harsh.

Since it came to power in May 2014, the BJP government has been making a host of pro-Hindu moves, like declaring a certain day in June as International Yoga Day. Going by the research of scholars such as Ruth Vanita and Devdutt Pattanaik (referred to earlier), legalizing homosexuality may also be construed by the government as a pro-Hindu move, given that the *Kamasutra* speaks of the *tritiya panthi* or third gender, and the Khajuraho temples display homoerotic sculpture. In fact, if the government seriously paid attention to the works of Ruth Vanita, Giti Thadani, and Devdutt Pattanaik, it would realize with a shock how anti-Hindu it has been all these years in its criminalization of homosexuality. Section 377 would have sung its swan song long ago.

The number 377 reminds me of another number, the number 175. This is because during the Nazi regime, Para 175 of the German Criminal Code, which was in force from 1871 to 1994, made homosexuality a crime (http://en.wikipedia. org/wiki/). The Nazis rigidly applied Para 175 not just to anal intercourse, but also to acts not involving physical contact, such as masturbating together in public washrooms. After that, the convictions increased tenfold, to about 8,000 per year. The Gestapo sent as many as 15,000 homosexual men to its concentration camps for "extermination through work." Most of them died there as a result of the torture and exhaustion.

In February 1933, the Nazi Party launched its 'purge' of 'homophiles', which was the term they used to describe gay, lesbian, and bisexual people. Underground gay groups were banned, books on homosexuality were burned, and homosexual men within the Nazi Party itself were killed. Kurt Hiller, the founder of the Hirschfield's Institute of Sex Research, was arrested and sent to a concentration camp. The Gestapo constituted a special division to compile lists of homophiles that were forced to conform to the German (heterosexual) norm. Those who were lucky managed to flee Germany. Those who could not escape became Hitler's holocaust victims, along with the Jews.

The Nazis were against gay men because they saw them as "subversives" who came in the way of their creation of a "master race." Heinrich Himmler, the leader of the Schutz Staffel (SS), glorified masculinity and the idea of a brotherhood among men. Homosexuality, according to him, violated these ideals. Himmler was alarmed that Germany had lost as many as four million men during the First World War, thus "upsetting the balance of the sexes in Germany." The need of the hour was for men to marry women and beget children, failing which the country was headed "for insignificance in fifty to one hundred years, [and] for burial in two hundred and fifty years".[1] Homosexuals were to be despised, for they were "no longer capable of having sex with a female." While sending homosexuals to concentration camps, leniency was displayed toward those who showed "Aryan-ness" (that is, coming from true Germanic stock), and to those who had managed to father children.

In the 12 years of Nazi rule between 1933 and 1945, as many as one 100,000 homosexual men were arrested by the Gestapo and the SS. Most of them were sent to regular prisons; however, as stated earlier, about 15,000 of them were sent to concentration camps. Statistics show that the death rate of homosexual men in the concentration camps was considerably higher—whilst about 60 percent of the homosexual prisoners died here, the figure for other prisoners has been roughly placed at 40 percent. This is because homophiles were treated unusually cruelly by their captors. They were persecuted not only by the German soldiers, but also by other prisoners whom the soldiers instigated. The persecution included sexual assault, highly plausible in the cramped concentration camps, in which, by 1945, the men were virtually sleeping on the wooden bunks one on top of the other. The SS made sure that the gay men in the camps were given more arduous and life-threatening work than the others. In the end, many of them were beaten to death. Those who did not die were used as guinea pigs by Nazi physicians to locate "a gay gene to cure any future Aryan children who were gay".[2] The SS men also used homosexual men for target practice, aiming their rifles at the downward pointing pink triangles that the latter were forced to wear around their necks. These pink triangles became the identification mark of homosexual prisoners, whose numbers

---

1 https://en.wikipedia.org/wiki/Persecution_of_homosexuals_in_Nazi_Germany_and_the_Holocaust, accessed June 9, 2017.

2 https://en.wikipedia.org/wiki/Persecution_of_homosexuals_in_Nazi_Germany_and_the_Holocaust, accessed June 9, 2017.

steadily rose from 170 in 1939 to over 600 by the end of the war in 1945. Like the Jews, the homosexuals belonged to assorted European nationalities, but the majority of them were Germans, French, Russians, and Poles. After the Stonewall Riot of 1969 in New York City, the pink triangle, which was once a hateful symbol of homosexual persecution, became its dazzling emblem. Today, to sport the pink triangle is not to remind oneself of the shameful excesses of the Nazis in the 1930s, but to announce one's (homo) sexuality to the world in a spirit of pride and defiance. Pink triangles are available in gay merchandize shops all over the Western world in the form of T-shirts and jewelry. They are a radical fashion statement.

After the war, East Germany reverted to the old version of the law, restricting the definition of homosexuality to anal intercourse. In 1968, homosexuality was made a punishable offence in Germany only if it involved a boy less than 18 years of age. In 1988, East Germany abolished the law altogether. West Germany, on the other hand, retained the Nazi law until 1973, revoking it altogether only in 1994, after the German reunification of 1989.

In 2002, the German government apologized to the gay community for its excesses during the Holocaust. A memorial, "To the gay and lesbian victims of National Socialism" stands in the city of Cologne today. It reads, *Totgeschlagen—Totgeschwiegen*, or "Struck Dead—Hushed Up."

After the Supreme Court's verdict on the reading down of Section 377, the petitioners and the gay community pinned their hopes on judicial remedies such as a review petition and a curative petition. The first of these was dismissed by a bench (with Justice Mukhopadhayay on it again), while the second has yet to come up for hearing in a meaningful way. Simultaneously, we dreamt of legislative redress, whereby Parliament itself will change the existing law by moving an amendment bill. The two Supreme Court judges, in fact, suggested this in their judgment, conveniently passing the buck on to the government. However, in spite of Sonia and Rahul Gandhi backing such a move, it is a pipe dream to expect Parliament to pass such an amendment. We all know of the buffoonery that ensued in Parliament on two consecutive days in 2015 when the Telangana Bill and the Jan Lokpal Bill came up respectively for discussion.

Yet, toward the end of November 2015, Finance Minister Arun Jaitley made a surprising statement at a literary festival. He said it was about time the Supreme Court abolished Section 377, because it "adversely affected millions of Indian citizens and their right to live a life of dignity and equality" (quoted widely in the media). I saw this as a conspiracy between the legislature and judiciary. For, just two years before Jaitley made his statement, the Supreme Court, recriminalizing homosexuality in India, said that it was not for the courts to decide on the constitutional validity of Section 377, but for the government. Now, this amounted to passing the buck between the legislature and the judiciary, and it made Jaitley's statement devious. As a member of the ruling party, and arguably the fourth most important man in the BJP government after Prime Minister Narendra Modi, BJP President Amit Shah, and Home Minister Rajnath Singh, all Jaitley needed to do, if he was serious about amending Section 377, was to implore his party to introduce a bill to that effect in Parliament. But this he chose not to do.

Let me elaborate on my conspiracy theory. It seems to me that both the legislature and the judiciary have entered into a pact to make polite noises about Section 377, knowing full well that at the end of the day neither of them wanted Section 377 to be amended, because it safeguarded the morals (and morality) of Indian society. The scrapping of Section 377 would also displease the Rashtriya Swayamsevak Sangh (RSS), the BJP's ideological mentor, as well as a whole host of other right-wing political outfits such as the Shiv Sena, the Maharashtra Navnirman Sena (MNS), the Vishwa Hindu Parishad (VHP), the

Hindu Mahasabha, and the Bajrang Dal, not to speak of Baba Ramdev.

As a member of Parliament, author Shashi Tharoor joined the band of voices against Section 377 by introducing two private member bills in Parliament to scrap Section 377, the first in December 2015, and the second, three months later, in March 2016. Both bills were rejected by Parliament. In the first case, Tharoor attributed the rejection (on FM radio) to a BJP member "who rounded up enough people to support him." While Tharoor got 24 members to support his bill, the BJP man got 70 members to oppose it. Tharoor said he wanted homosexuality to be decriminalized "because it brought India to the 21st century." Tharoor was asked why his party, the Congress, did nothing to amend Section 377 when it was in power. To this, his reply was that the Congress had "no time to introduce the bill in Parliament between December 2013 [when the Supreme Court judgment came out] and May 2014, when the new government came to power." Tharoor called the BJP the enemy. He said, "As far as I am concerned, this is not just about one particular [sexual] practice, as the enemy is portraying. Instead, it is about the freedom guaranteed by the Constitution of India." Tharoor was bothered by the fact that if a person belonged to a different sexual orientation, he could be harassed. He pointed out that since the December 2013 judgment, 578 gay men were arrested under Section 377. Tharoor was asked what his next step would be. He said he would reintroduce the bill in the next session of Parliament.

In March 2016, Tharoor kept his word and reintroduced the bill. But it got rejected again, with just 18 members voting in favour of it and 58 members voting against it. Tharoor attributed this to the low turnout of MPs (including Congress MPs) who did not show up in Parliament on a Friday afternoon, when private member bills came up for discussion. However, he had burnt his bridges. He realized that the parliamentary route was not the route to be taken to scrap Section 377.

Earlier, participating in a TV debate on NewsX channel, in which his opponents were the lawyers Anjali Gopalan of the Naz Foundation and Colin Gonsalves, BJP minister Subramaniam Swamy challenged his own party colleague Arun Jaitley, who wanted the Supreme Court to repeal Section 377. Swamy dared Jaitley to express this view at a party meeting, implying that Jaitley and his party were not on the same page on this. According to Swamy, homosexuality was against Indian culture. This, in a way, was fielded by Tharoor later, who pointed out that homosexuality was represented in ancient Indian texts like the *Kamasutra*, as well as in the temple sculptures of Khajuraho, Konark, and Hampi. Nor was there any evidence of its being outlawed and criminalized in precolonial India. Instead, it was criminalized and outlawed by the English Victorians in the 19th century. Then how could Subramaniam Swamy say that homosexuality was against Indian culture? Tharoor commented on the paradox that the BJP, which thought of itself as the custodian of Hinduism and Hindutva, was actually being anti-Hindu and pro-colonial in its approach to homosexuality. Other scholars have pointed this out too, and this has been referred to earlier in this chapter. Extending his fallacious argument that homosexuality was against Indian culture, Swamy claimed that the people of India did not want homosexuality to be legalized. But this, obviously, was not based on statistical evidence. However, even if what Swamy claimed here was taken to be true, it was evident that the people of India were victims of the same amnesia (in relation to the culture of precolonial India) that afflicted Swamy. They needed to be educated. In the past, it was through education that the people of India realized that *sati* and child marriage were evils that needed to be abolished. They needed to be similarly educated about discrimination based on one's sexual orientation. In the debate, Swamy echoed Baba Ramdev when he said that homosexuality would lead to bestiality (see Chapter VII). What both Swamy and Ramdev failed to realize was that we are talking here of consensual homosexuality. Animals cannot give their consent to human beings to have sex with them because they (animals) do not have agency. When Gopalan and Collins pointed out to Swamy that homosexuality (like heterosexuality) was about love, and not just about sex, he said, "I love my dog. That does not mean I can have sex with it." This was not just untenable; it was shocking in its absurdity. For some strange reason, Subramaniam Swamy also associated the legalizing of homosexuality with the proliferation of gay bars. This was a trivialization of the issue as well as a perpetuation of stereotypes. Swamy's unkindest cut came in his slanderous references to Shashi Tharoor. When the NewsX anchor asked Swamy what he thought of Tharoor's private member bill to amend Section 377, he sniggered and asked why Tharoor was so interested in getting Section 377 repealed. Then, without provocation, Swamy referred to Tharoor's dead wife Sunanda Pushkar. I wondered whether Swamy was trying to make a specious connection between Sunanda Pushkar's alleged suicide and Shashi Tharoor's sexuality.

The RSS too stepped into the debate when Rakesh Sinha claimed in another TV programme on the same channel (NewsX) that Shashi Tharoor introduced the private member bill in Parliament because he was of a "European mindset." Thus, to him, as to Subramaniam Swamy, homosexuality was a European phenomenon. However, even if that were so, there are enough Indians of a European mindset for the government to consider abolishing Section 377. When the television anchor asked Sinha whether Arun Jaitley was also of a European mindset, since it was he who wanted the Supreme Court to repeal Section 377, the former was flabbergasted, hard put for an answer. Surely no BJP member could be said to have that most degenerate of things—a European mindset. Rakesh Sinha's uninformed view is contradicted by what Saleem Kidawai says on the subject, namely that homosexuality existed in medieval India as well. Kidwai writes, "During the early medieval period, there are a few scattered references to same-sex love, while in the late medieval period, a huge body of literature on same-sex love develops" (Vanita and Kidwai, 2000: 107). Next, Rakesh Sinha came up with his ultimate gem. He claimed that it was not the people of India who wanted Section 377 to be abolished. Rather, it was the people of the West who wanted it gone, and not for human rights reasons, but because it came in the way of their pedophilic and pornographic activities in the country. Once homosexuality was legalized, they would not face the risk of going to prison.

Some months later, another RSS man, Dattatreya Hosabale, who was Deputy General Secretary of the party, said that homosexuality was not criminal behavior, and so it was wrong to criminalize it. However, he clarified that though, to him, homosexuality was not criminal, it was immoral and patho-logical. This, of course, was specious reasoning, typical of the RSS and other right-wing outfits. When a TV channel asked BJP spokesperson Shaina N. C. to comment on Hosabale's position, she suggested that Hosabale was merely being cautious. To support her argument, she cited Shashi Tharoor's March 2016 private member bill to amend Section 377 (referred to earlier) that met with few takers. It was surprising that Shaina, a BJP spokesperson, should even mention the name of a member of her party's sworn enemy, the Congress. Responding to Hosabale's claim that homosexuality was immoral, and junk-ing his claims, Vivek Dewan, a lawyer and gay rights activist, pointed out that there was no crisis of morality in India when the Delhi High Court read down Section 377 in July 2009, so that consenting adult homosexuals were excluded from the purview of the law. Whereas, Harish Iyer said that once Section 377 was repealed, our "sisters and daughters" would no longer be deceived by the parents of gay men who thrust their sons on them.

Where there is a will there is a way. This old adage was proved in Parliament when it passed the amended Juvenile

Justice Bill in December 2015. The new law made teenage boys between the ages of sixteen and eighteen culpable for heinous crimes, making it possible for them to be tried as adults. Though the bill met with considerable opposition from child rights activists, Parliament passed it nonetheless. And it was passed almost overnight. Now the question is, if Parliament could pass the Juvenile Justice Bill so soon, why could not it amend Section 377 with equal speed? Why did it dither on it? The only answer to this is that Parliament is discriminatory. It could empathize with the suffering of Jyoti Singh (Nirbhaya) whose brutal December 2012 rape and murder led to the introduction of the Juvenile Justice Bill. But it could not empathize with the suffering of thousands of gays and transgenders—India's Matthew Shepards—who are the victims of brutality and harassment on a daily basis. What Parliament needs to realize is that Section 377 of the IPC is lethal. If a gay man is murdered because of his sexuality, the Section even makes it possible for a good lawyer to free the murderer on the ground that the murder was committed in order to 'cleanse' society, and was motivated by the highest moral values.

As for the judiciary, the February 2016 hearing of the curative petition, filed by the Naz Foundation and others against the December 2013 judgment, turned out to be a damp squib. It was a cruel kindling of our hopes, for all we were told was that a five-judge bench would hear all the eight curative petitions connected to the case *at some future date*. However, no time frame was spelt out for the hearing of the petitions. It seemed as if the Supreme Court was merely buying time. Meanwhile, we were back to square one, with LGBT people in the country facing the risk of blackmail, arrest, homophobia, and gay bashing. The choice of coming out of the closet or staying in it was, to us, like choosing between the devil and the deep blue sea. Both courses of action could be equally perilous. The Supreme Court also did not constitute the promised five-judge bench. This is important, because the fate of the case depends on the mindset of the judges. Apparently, in a curative petition, the judges who heard the original case are supposed to be a part of the larger bench hearing the curative petition. Of course, this will not apply to our curative petition as both the judges who heard the original case have retired.

It is intriguing why Supreme Court judges cannot be unanimous about the constitutional validity (or otherwise) of Section 377. In a newspaper interview given to *The Indian Express* in January 2016, Justice Vikramjit Sen, who retired after a short three-year term as Supreme Court judge, commented on the validity of Section 377. He said, "Why do a penal law and a court have to regulate what you do in private?" The judge was of the view that personal (sexual) choices were valid as long as they did not infringe anyone else's rights. Yet, as a Supreme Court judge himself, Justice Sen was more inclined to side with the judiciary than the legislature. He wondered why the government had not taken a call on Section 377 till the present time, although the Supreme Court had asked them to do so way back in December 2013. The judge felt that it was Parliament's job to get rid of archaic laws. He said, "I agree with the view that the lawmakers have the primary duty to appreciate the changing times and make the right decision to protect the rights of all groups." But Justice Sen was also critical of the judiciary. In a veiled reference to the December 2013 judgment that reinstated Section 377, he argued that when the Supreme Court had, from time to time, consciously interfered with various policy decisions of the government, and had read down various irrelevant laws or had held them to be unconstitutional, "there was no impediment for the bench concerned to exercise its power in respect of Section 377 too." Citing his own example, Justice Sen said that when he was Chief Justice of the Karnataka High Court in 2012, he employed, for the first time, a transgender person as a court employee. In his own words, "People questioned my decision but I am proud of my call. And today, that person has impressed everyone with his skill and dedication."

In December 2015, I was on a panel to discuss the "Section 377 Impasse" at the Goa Arts and Literature Festival. Both my co-panelists, Nandita Haskar and Jason Keith Fernandes, came from a human rights background. They asked me whether Section 377 concerned only the gay community in India, or was it a reprehensible law that bothered everyone who stood up for human rights. What they were really lamenting was the fact that our agendas had become too narrow. Each marginalized group had become so myopic that it could not see beyond its own immediate concerns. There was no attempt on the part of the groups to build coalitions with other groups. However, I pointed out to my co-panelists that the gay community was at the receiving end here. While we were certainly willing to broaden our support base by building coalitions with other groups such as the feminists and the Dalits, it was they who kept away from us, possibly because our cause had to do with sex. This was proved during the JNU protests of February and March 2016, when some JNU students allegedly issued a statement saying, if Section 377 can be debated in Parliament, why cannot Afzal Guru's hanging. The implications of this statement, according to me, were that Section 377 was a less legitimate issue than the Kashmir problem, with which Afzal Guru's hanging was connected. Human rights should concern all sections of society, regardless of what our separate agendas are. However, there is a tendency to prioritize human rights, with some issues taken to be more important than others. In such a fallacious classification, the rights of sexual minorities are always at the bottom of the ladder. One reason for this is that LGBT people in India comprise, may be, less than 2 percent of the overall population. Whereas, other constituencies concerned with caste, class, gender, and ethnicity issues have a much larger membership. However, as explained earlier, a more insidious reason is that the demands of the LGBT community have to do with sex, which in turn has to do with morality. In short, the demands of LGBT people are often seen as immoral. The alleged statement by some JNU students, referred to above, meant that to them the business of an independent homeland for the Kashmiri people (for which Afzal Guru died) was entirely different from the business of sexual preference. For, while human beings cannot live without a homeland, they can certainly live without sex. Religion and sexuality are strange bedfellows. In 2015, when I gave a talk on the late poet Agha Shahid Ali at Kashmir University, Srinagar, my hosts forbade me from making a mention of the poet's homosexuality. I found this strange, considering that Agha Shahid Ali was as much of a poet expressing his longing for (male) companionship as he expressed his longing for a free homeland. Why is it that the people of Kashmir wanted me to concentrate not on the former but only on the latter? The JNU students were supposed to be anti-establishment. Thus, it was out of character for them to pit Afzal Guru against Section 377. Both Afzal Guru and the LGBT community in India are outlaws. Our goals may be different but we are outlaws all the same. So, shouldn't we be speaking of a coalition of outlawed persons? If there is a witch hunt for militants, there is equally a witch hunt for homosexuals.

Toward the end of the year 2015, the Bollywood film star Aamir Khan spoke of leaving India, given the (unspoken) fact that he was a Muslim, and India was ruled by a Hindu fundamentalist party that was intolerant toward Muslims and other minorities. The Government of India immediately accused Aamir Khan of sedition. I responded to Aamir Khan's statement and the government's reaction in informal conversations, pointing out that the LGBT community in India would be happy to leave the country, given the fact that Section 377 made us criminals in our own country, while even a neighboring country like Nepal (a Hindu nation at that) had decriminalized homosexuality.

I said, given a chance, we would much rather immigrate to a country where the laws of the land were in our favour. These countries could be (other than Nepal) the UK, the USA, France, Germany, Spain, and South Africa. It was obvious that we would live happier lives in these countries than back home in India. However, as far as the Government of India was concerned, for LGBT people to speak of leaving India was obviously not the same as Aamir Khan speaking of it. We would not merely be called seditionists. On the contrary, the Government of India would be glad that we were leaving, for it would help them to 'cleanse' the nation.

Bibliography

Books

Akhavi, Negar, ed. 2008. *Aids Sutra: Untold Stories from India*. New Delhi: Random House India.

Baker, Steven and Rohit K. Dasgupta, eds. 2013. *Popular Masculine Cultures in India: Critical Essays*. Kolkata: Setu Prakashani.

Barthes, Roland. 1977. *Roland Barthes*. Trans. Richard Howard. New York: Hill and Wang.

Bose, Brinda, and Subhabrata Bhattacharyya, eds. 2007. *The Phobic and the Erotic: The Politics of Sexualities in Contemporary India*. Calcutta: Seagull Books.

Butler, Judith. 1990. *Gender Trouble: Feminism and the Subversion of Identity*. New York: Routledge.

Chaudhuri, Rosinka, ed. 2016. *A History of Indian Poetry in English*. London: Cambridge University Press.

de Beauvoir, Simone. 1950. *The Second Sex*. London: Vintage Classics.

Devy, G. N. 1992. *After Amnesia: Tradition and Change in Indian Literary Criticism*. Bombay: Orient Longman.

Dollimore, Jonathan. 1991. *Sexual Dissidence: Augustine to Wilde, Freud to Foucault*. Oxford: Clarendon Press.

Duggan, Lisa. 2003. *Twilight of Equality: Neoliberalism, Cultural Politics and the Attack on Democracy*. Boston: Beacon Press.

Dworkin, Andrea. 1987. *Intercourse*. New York: Free Press.

Fuss, Diana. 1989. *Essentially Speaking: Feminism, Nature and Difference*. New York: Routledge.

Ghosh, Subhagata, ed. 2015. *Selected Swakanthey: Reflections on Non-normative Gender–Sexual Issues and Lives*. Kolkata: Sappho for Equality.

Gokhale, Sandhya. 2006. *Quest* (Screenplay). Bombay: Popular Prakashan.

Goldie, Terry. 2008. *Queersexlife: Autobiographical Notes on Sexuality, Gender and Identity*. Vancouver: Arsenal Pulp Press.

Grossman, Andrew, ed. 2000. *Queer Asian Cinema: Shadows in the Shade.* New York: Haworth Press.

Hajratwala, Minal, ed. 2012. *Out: Stories from the New Queer India.* Bombay: Queer Ink.

Halberstam, Jack. 2011. *The Queer Art of Failure.* Durham: Duke University Press.

Kapur, Manju. 2004. *A Married Woman.* London: Faber and Faber.

King, Bruce. 2001. *Modern Indian Poetry in English.* New Delhi: Oxford University Press.

Kureishi, Hanif. 1986. *My Beautiful Laundrette and The Rainbow Sign.* London: Faber and Faber.

Law, Benjamin. 2013. *Gaysia: Adventures in the Queer East.* New Delhi: Random House India.

Lotringer, Sylvere, ed. 1996. "History and Homosexuality." In *Foucault Live: Interviews 1961–1984* [Semiotext(e)/Foreign Agents]. Translated by Lysa Hochroth and John Johnston. New York: MIT Press.

Mehrotra, Arvind Krishna, ed. 1992. *The Oxford Anthology of Twelve Modern Indian Poets.* New Delhi: Oxford University Press.

Menon, Nivedita. 2012. *Seeing Like a Feminist.* New Delhi: Zubaan–Penguin.

Merchant, Hoshang, ed. 1999. *Yaraana: Gay Writing from India.* New Delhi: Penguin Books.

Merchant, Hoshang. 2009. *Forbidden Sex/Forbidden Texts: New India's Gay Poets.* New Delhi: Routledge.

Naik, M. K. 1982. *A History of Indian English Literature.* New Delhi: Sahitya Akademi.

Naik, M. K., and Shyamala Narayan. 2011. *Indian English Literature 1980–2000: A Critical Survey.* New Delhi: Pencraft International.

Narrain, Arvind, and Gautam Bhan, eds. 2005. *Because I Have a Voice: Queer Politics in India.* New Delhi: Yoda Press.

Pattanaik, Devdutt. 2014. *Shikhandi And Other Tales They Don't Tell You.* New Delhi: Zubaan–Penguin.

Rao, R. Raj. 2001. *One Day I Locked My Flat in Soul City.* New Delhi: HarperCollins.

———. 2003. *The Boyfriend.* New Delhi: Penguin Books India.

———. 2006. *BomGay.* New Delhi: Aark Arts.

———. and Dibyajyoti Sarma, eds. 2009. *Whistling in the Dark: Twenty One Queer Interviews.* New Delhi: SAGE.

Ramachandran, Raju. "One Court, Two Mindsets." *The Indian Express.* April 18, 2014.

Ratti, Rakesh, ed. 1993. *A Lotus of Another Color: An Unfolding of the South Asian Gay and Lesbian Experience.* Boston: Alyson Publications Inc.

Revathi, A. 2010. *The Truth About Me: A Hijra Life Story.* Trans. V. Geetha. New Delhi: Penguin Books.

Rushdie, Salman. 1982. *Midnight's Children.* New York: Avon Books.

Ryan, Barbara. 2001. *Identity Politics in the Women's Movement.* New York: NYU Press.

Sedgwick, Eve Kosofsky. 1990. *Epistemology of the Closet*. Berkley and Los Angeles: University of California Press.

Sen, Vikramjit. Interview. *The Indian Express*. January 2016.

Sukhbir Singh, ed. 2014. *Gay Subcultures and Literatures: The Indian Projections*. Shimla: Indian Institute of Advanced Studies.

Sukthankar, Ashwini. 1999. *Facing the Mirror: Lesbian Writing from India*. New Delhi: Penguin Books.

Talwar, Rajesh. 2013. *Courting Injustice*. New Delhi: Hay House.

Traub,Valeried, and Halperin, David M., eds. 2009. *Gay Shame*. Chicago: Chicago University Press.

Tripathi, Laxminarayan. 2015. *Me Hijra, Me Laxmi*. Trans. R. Raj Rao and P. G. Joshi. New Delhi: Oxford University Press.

Vanita, Ruth, and Saleem Kidwai, eds. 2010. *Same-Sex Love in India: Readings from Literature and History*. New Delhi: Macmillan India Ltd.

_____ ed. 2002. *Queering India: Same-Sex Love and Eroticism in Indian Culture and Society*. New York: Routledge.

_____ 2005. *Love's Rite: Same-Sex Marriage in India and the West*. New Delhi: Penguin Books.

Varghese, Abraham. 1994. *My Own Country: A Doctor's Story of a Town and its People in the Age of Aids*. New York: Vintage Books.

Warner, Michael, and Lauren Berlant. 1999. "Sex in Public" in *The Culture Studies Reader*. Ed. Simon During. London: Routledge.

Films

Fire, Dir. Deepa Mehta, 1996.

Quest, Dir. Amol Palekar, 2006

Montreal Main, Dir. Frank Vitale, 1974

No Easy Walk to Freedom, Dir. Nancy Nicol, 2014

Dostana, Dir. Karan Johar, 2008

BomGay, Dir. Riyad Wadia, 1996

Project Bolo, Dir. Sridhar Rangayan, 2012

Aligarh, Dir. Hansal Mehta, 2016

Sholay, Dir. Ramesh Sippy, 1975

Brokeback Mountain, Dir. Ang Lee, 2005

Shamitabh, Dir. R. Balki, 2015

Sairat, Dir. Nagraj Manjule, 2016.

Internet Sites

https://en.wikipedia.org/wiki/Persecution_of_homosexuals_in_Nazi_Germany_and_the_Holocaust

Matthew Shepard. http://en.wikipedia.org/wiki

Index

About the Author

R. Raj Rao is a writer, poet, and teacher of literature and 'one of India's leading gay-rights activists'. His 2003 novel, *The Boyfriend*, is one of the first gay novels to come from India. Rao was one of the first recipients of the newly established Quebec-India awards.

R. Raj Rao is the author of almost a dozen books of poetry, fiction, plays, biography, and criticism. His book, *Whistling in the Dark: Twenty-one Queer Interviews*, co-edited with Dibyajyoti Sarama, was published by SAGE in 2009. He is former Professor and Head of the Department of English at the Savitribai Phule Pune University.

I-135/16